Learning

to Create Your First Web Page

with 100 Practical Exercises

Learning

to Create Your First Web Page

with 100 Practical Exercises

www.mcb-press.com

Learning to Create Your First Web Page with 100 Practical Exercises

Copyright © 2013 MEDIAactive

First edition: 2013

Published by © MCB Press, distributed in USA and Canada by ATLAS BOOKS 30 Amberwood Parkway, Ashland, Ohio 44805. To contact a representative, please e-mail us at order@bookmasters.com.

www.mcb-press.com

Cover Designer: Ndenu

ISBN: 978-84-267-2008-5

Printed in EU

DL: B-21369-2013

Printed by Publidisa

Presentation

LEARNING TO CREATE YOUR FIRST WEB PAGE WITH 100 PRACTICAL EXERCISES

These 100 practical exercises take you through the process of creating a free web page using the services of Blogger, WordPress.com, and Facebook. They will also teach you to enhance your social media plan using services such as Twitter, Instagram, Pinterest, and Foursquare, which allow you to create links, strengthen your brand, and build relationships with both current and potential clients. While it is impossible to list all the possible social networks in this book, we have chosen those that are essential for small businesses that want to move forward with Web 2.0. Once you complete the 100 exercises, you will be able to communicate through the social networking environment in a solid and coherent way.

THE LEARNING METHOD

Our experience in the field of education has led us to design this type of manual, where each function is taught by working through a practical exercise. Each exercise is explained step-by-step and click by click so that they are easy to follow and complete. We have also illustrated the most important steps with both descriptive images as well as the expected results. The notes marked IMPORTANT offer complementary information about the topics dealt with in the exercises.

Thanks to this system, once the 100 exercises have been completed, you will be able to use the most popular social network tools confidently and get the most out of their many features.

WHO THIS MANUAL IS FOR

This book is intended for self-employed professionals who want to promote their work and small businesses that would like to become better known and establish new forms of communication. This book emphasizes the process of creating web pages (in blog format), as well as linking the pages with other social networking sites and the use of the latter for commercial means. If you already use social media on a personal level, you know it is very useful for keeping track of certain things, and this book will give you tips on how to transition from personal use to business use.

Although each exercise is treated separately, we recommend that you work through the book, given that many of the exercises are to be worked through progressively and sequentially on the same page or profile. In addition, we have grouped together exercises with a common theme. However, the exercises are also independent and should you need information on a certain topic, you can go directly to the exercise that covers the subject and apply the information to your own project.

HOW TO CREATE YOUR FIRST WEB PAGE

This manual will teach you how to create a blog with two of the free service global leaders, Blogger and WordPress.com. You will be able to add new pages to form a true structured page, customize it, add applications or widgets as required, and publish all kinds of content.

You will also learn to use Facebook as a true professional, you will be able to turn your personal profile into a business page, create advertisements, promote events, and tell the story of your business through text and all kinds of multimedia content.

You will become addicted to the immediacy of Twitter's 140 characters, and you will be able to share your everyday life through Instagram's spectacular images, build a corporate image using Pinterest, and publicize your business with Foursquare. You will even be able to use all of these tools from your cell phone.

How *Learning...* books work

The title of each exercise concisely expresses what it is about. Thus, if you are interested, you can go directly to the action you want to learn or review.

The exercises have been systematically written step-by-step, so that you will never get lost during their execution.

The number on the right-hand side of each page clearly indicates which exercise you are on.

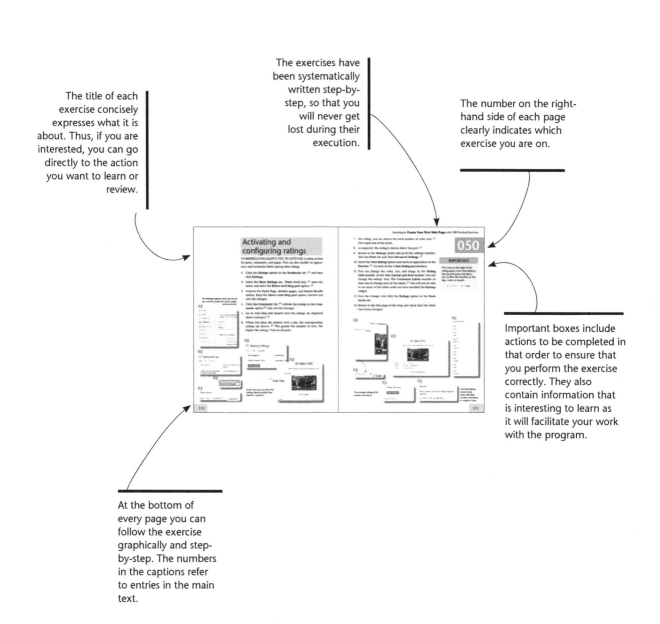

Important boxes include actions to be completed in that order to ensure that you perform the exercise correctly. They also contain information that is interesting to learn as it will facilitate your work with the program.

At the bottom of every page you can follow the exercise graphically and step-by-step. The numbers in the captions refer to entries in the main text.

Table of contents

Table of contents

A tour of the different Web 2.0 resources

SOCIAL NETWORKS ARE MAINLY BASED ON the Internet and are used by all types of people. Social networks have changed the way we communicate. They are powerful tools that are often free, and are available to small businesses and professionals who are self-employed and would like to publicize their work. This first lesson will give you a short introduction to the most relevant resources available today.

1. A variety of services allow you to create free websites with a relative degree of customization without requiring a high level of technical knowledge. Blogs have great potential to attract new users or clients, to gain a high profile, and to communicate with the general public and potential clients. With this manual you will learn how to create and manage one using Blogger [1] and WordPress.com [2] although there are other similar services, with fewer features such as BitaCoras (http://bitacoras.com/bitacorae), Obolog (www. obolog.com), Over-Blog (http://es.overblog.com), or Blogia (www.blogia.com) [3].

2. Social networks or social media, meanwhile, help us to advertise services and products and to interact with customers. Of the Social networks, used for leisure and the development of social relationships, Facebook [4] is the current leader, al-

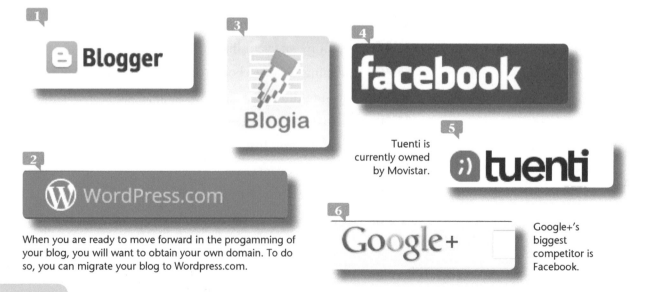

When you are ready to move forward in the progamming of your blog, you will want to obtain your own domain. To do so, you can migrate your blog to Wordpress.com.

Tuenti is currently owned by Movistar.

Google+'s biggest competitor is Facebook.

though we should not fail to take into consideration others such as the Spanish Tuenti, [5] which has 14 million users and is experiencing massive growth, and is aimed at a younger demographic (those under 35). Neither should we lose sight of Google+, [6] wich is trying to gain ground on Facebook. For companies, this type of social network is an excellent way to forge links with users and followers, to disseminate information, or to share videos and photographs.

3. Microblogging has become synonymous with Twitter, [7] the network of the 140 characters, although other networks also exist such as Tumblr, [8] which is a hybrid that permits the sharing of multimedia content, its own and that of others, or Pinterest, [9] which focuses mainly on image-based communication.

4. If you would like to publish multimedia material, you should consider using pages such as Flikr [10] and, the aforementioned, Pinterest for sharing photographs. Instagram [11] can be used if you would like to explain your daily activities through photographs, and YouTube [12], as well as Vimeo and Blip.tv can be used to share videos.

5. If you offer your services or product from a physical location, you cannot ignore the so-called proximity networks, among which we point out Foursquare, [13] which is featured in this manual, Yelp, or Google Places, which helps you to appear in Google Maps searches.

001

IMPORTANT

If you wish to strengthen your professional relationships, promote your work, and update yourself, you must have a profile on a professional network. The best known example is LinkedIn, a leader in this sector, although Xing is also well considered in certain sectors.

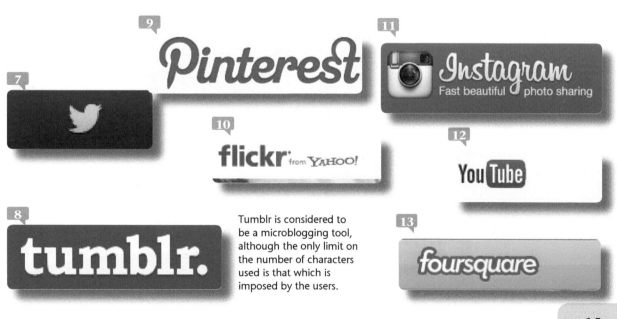

Tumblr is considered to be a microblogging tool, although the only limit on the number of characters used is that which is imposed by the users.

Creating a Blogger Account

BLOGGER, AS WE HAVE ALREADY SAID, is a free and very intuitive service that allows you to create, publish, and manage your own personal web page or blog simply and efficiently. In the following exercises we will see how to create a blog with Blogger and, of course, how to get the most out of it.

1. To create a blog in Blogger, the first thing you need is a Google Account. If you do not already have one, go to the home page (**www.blogger.com**), click on the **sign up** button, and fill in the form. Create your Google Account. The same account can be used for Gmail, Google+, and YouTube, among others. If you already have a Google Account, you can either enter through it or directly via the Blogger page.

2. Blogger's welcome page displays a preview of your profile, which will appear on all Google products and the Web. Click on the link **View my complete profile**.

3. If you wish to change one of the photographs, you need only place the pointer over the image and click the link that appears. Do so with the profile photo on the right-hand side.

4. As the pointer is placed over it, the text **Change profile photo** appears, and on clicking it the box, **select profile photo** opens, which will allow you to upload a photograph from

You do not need a new Google Account if you already have one.

the desktop (using the option **Upload**), choose an image from your albums (**Your Photos**) of photos, which are labled (**Photos of you**), or take a new photo (**Web camera**).

5. For this exercise, simply open a file dialog box on your computer and drag the image that you would like to set as your profile photo to the central box where you see the words **Drag photos here**, [4] and when the image loads, [5] click the link **Creative Kit**.

6. Your profile photo can be edited from here. Select the **Crop** option that activates a cutting grid and then, by dragging the corners, select the area of the photo that you would like to use. Click on the **Apply** button. [6]

7. You will see four tabs that allow you to activate various options. Select the **Effects** tab and, if you wish, apply one of the options. Once done you can modify it [7] by using the controls. Then click on the **Save** button that you will find at the top right-hand corner. Adjust the crop area, if necessary, and click the **Set as Profile Photo** button to save it.

8. A dialog box will open where you can add text to share on the network. For this exercise click **Cancel**.

9. Close the profile window where you could add comments, and in Blogger's welcome page click the **Continue to Blogger** button. [8]

Creating a blog in Blogger

ONCE YOU HAVE SET UP YOUR profile, Google can create a blog in exactly three steps. You only need to click the button New Blog on the Blogger Desktop, introduce a title and an available address, choose a template, and click the button Create Blog.

1. The page that you left on the screen after completing the previous exercise is the **Blogger Dashboard**. In the upper section that now indicates that you do not have any blogs, a list of blogs will be created. The next section called **Reading List** will list all the blogs you follow. You can edit its configuration, add new blogs, and manage the list. To do so you must click the button in the shape of a cog on the top right-hand side of the Dashboard. 🖵 The blog **Blogger Buzz** has been added by default. This is a blog from the Blogger service that allows the user to remain up to date with any new developments. Click the button **New Blog** in the upper section to create your first blog now.

2. To begin you must give the blog a title, which will appear in the page's header (it is not the same as the address). Think about it well as this will be how you present yourself. Remem-

Once you have created or edited your Google profile, you can create your first blog.

Title

Nourishes all

Blogs List › Create a new blog

| Title | Nourishes all |
| Address | nourishesall .blogspot.com |

This blog address is available.

Template

Dynamic Views   Simple   Picture Window

ber that you will be able to change it later on for another one. Type the chosen title into the field. 2

3. Now, in the second field, you should type the address at which your blog can be reached from any navigator. Keep in mind that it should be easy to remember, and it is advisable to avoid using special characters. If the web will be the communication channel of a business, use its name as part of the address. As you write the text, an alert will indicate whether that address is available or if it is already being used by another blog. 3 To be able to use an address, the text **This blog address is available** will appear.

4. When you have found an address that you are happy with, choose one of the templates that the service offers. Although this first dialog box offers just a few options, you will be able to choose from many more templates later on, just as it says at the bottom of the box. You will also be able to personalize the pre-designed templates.

5. Once you have selected a template, simply click the button **Create blog!** 4

The Blogger Dashboard will appear again where you will see the new blog, which, obviously and as is indicated, does not yet have any posts. 5

The Blogger Dashboard allows easy access to all of the user's blogs, as well as a way to manage the posts in each of them. For the moment, as no posts have been published, it is empty.

Creating your first post in Blogger

BLOGGER HAS A TEXT EDITOR DESIGNED for introducing on-line texts, but we shall see that there are other methods to post an article. If you prefer, you can enter text in any application of your choice and paste it into the Blogger editor to then post it.

1. You have already created a blog so it is time to start adding content. For the moment there are a couple of ways to do so: Clicking on the **Start blogging** link or on the **Create new post** button, which is orange with a white pencil icon. Use either of the two links now.

2. The **Blogger Post editor** opens. It is a simple text editor that we will work with more in the next exercises. For now, click in the **Post title** field and enter the text that will be used as the title of your post.

3. Now write a few test sentences in the text field.

4. To check how the content will appear, click on **Preview**.

5. A new preview window of the blog opens showing the post's exact appearance once it is published. The turning cogs indi-

All of the blogs created with the active profile are shown on the Blogger Dashboard.

· Post We eat what we digest

Before posting an article, you can see a preview and make all necessary adjustments.

20

cate that this is just a preview as the post has not yet been published. 🔳

6. Close the window to return to the Post editor.

7. You can also copy a text written with any application into the editor. For this exercise download the Word document WHAT WE DIGEST FEEDS US.docx, and open it. For the same purpose you can also use any text document that includes different styles (bold, italic, etc.).

8. Select and copy the whole text and return to the Blogger editor.

9. Select the test sentence that you inserted a few steps ago and paste the copied text over it. You can use either the shortcut **Ctrl + V** or the **Paste** option from the navigator's Edit button. 🔳

10. Observe that the text has been pasted maintaining the original attributes but not the font. Let's post it now. Click the **Publish** button. 🔳

11. Once the article has been uploaded, a window opens inviting the user to share with their Google contacts, a circle or an e-mail address. For this exercise, just click the button **Cancel**. 🔳

IMPORTANT

When you publish a post in Blogger, you can share it directly through Google+ (Google's social network) or through an e-mail address.

7

Share on Google+   Paul Adams

We eat what we digest »
We eat what we digest Just as food is the process by which eat certain products, nutrition is the process that allows us to take advantage of the nutrients in these foods. Although they are closely

---

4

Nourishes all

WEDNESDAY, JANUARY 9, 2013

We eat what we digest

Just as food is the process by which eat certain products, nutrition is the process that allows us to take advantage of the nutrients in these foods. Although they are closely related, are not synonymous and, sometimes, not products we eat nourish us in the best way.

Posted by Paul Adams at 6.32 AM

No comments:

Post a Comment

ABOUT ME

Paul Adams
View my complete profile

Content can be copied and pasted using the traditional shortcuts or using the corresponding options from the navigator's **Edit** menu.

5

Edit	View	Favorites	Tools	Help
Cut				Ctrl+X
Copy				Ctrl+C
Paste				Ctrl+V
Select all				Ctrl+A
Find on this page...				Ctrl+F

Publish

6

Nourishes all · Post   We eat what we digest   Publish   Save   Preview

Compose   HTML   ↶   *f* ▾ ᴛ̅ ▾ Normal   ▾ **B** *I* U ᴬᴮᶜ A ▾ ✎ ▾ **Link** 🖼 🎬 ≡

We eat what we digest

*Just as **food** is the process by which eat certain products, **nutrition** is the process that allows us to take advantage of the nutrients in these foods. Although they are closely related, are not synonymous and, sometimes, not products we eat nourish us in the best way.*

Nutrition is the action through which extract, transform and use nutrients from the foods we eat. It is an autonomous process in which we can not influence directly but indirectly, because the power itself is or should be a conscious process.

To lose weight is very important that food is based on highly nutritious food and be able to digest efficiently, since not all the food we eat are able to nourish equally. For example, foods that are indigestible and that we reach the large intestine partially digested eventually rotting and can not be utilized properly. Generally, natural foods are not indigestible for themselves, unless they are ingested in large amounts, but in fact there are people who are intolerant of certain products and it is important to be able to identify and eliminate them from your diet. Natural foods usually are not

When text is copied from Word, its text attributes are maintained, although the code may contain errors.

Editing a Blogger post (I)

IMPORTANT

By default, Blogger uses a **WYSIWYG** (What you see is what you get) text editor. Thus, the appearance of any text, images, or videos that you might insert into it is very similar to that of the final published material.

ONCE YOU HAVE PUBLISHED A POST in a blog you can open it again in Blogger's blog editor. You need only open the Posts file and indicate that you wish to edit it. In this way you will, once again, have access to all of the editing tools on this page. In this exercise we will work with some of them.

1. On publishing a post Blogger will send you back to its **Dashboard**.  Click the link that shows the number of posts, which should now be 1.

2. This way you can access the **Posts** file where you will see the title that you created in the previous exercise. Place the pointer over it.

3. Four options will appear: **Edit**, **View**, **Share**, **Delete**. Click the first option.

4. You will find yourself, again, in Blogger's **blog editor** where you can make any modification. To begin, select and erase the title from the main body of text as it is repeated. Also erase the line that contains it.

5. Open the **Edit** menu and select the **Select all** option.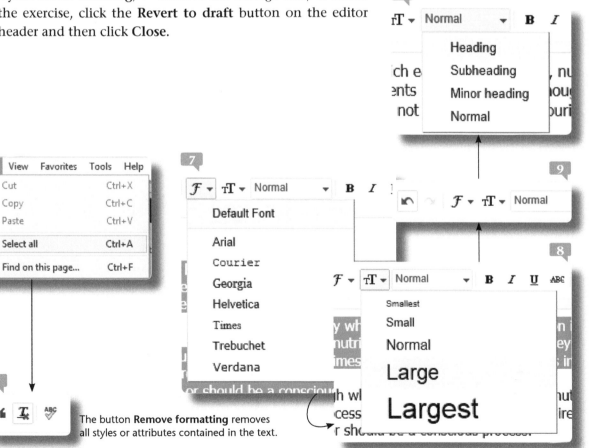

6. You could also use the keyboard shortcut that appears next to the option. Now press **Remove formatting**. This is the last button on the **Editor's** toolbar and is a T crossed with a small X.

7. Click the **Font** button (the icon is a letter F) and use the drop-down menu to see the available font styles.

8. Select the **Default font** option to apply the one that is the default for the theme used.

9. Select the first paragraph and click the next button, **Font size**, and choose the **Large** option.

10. The text changes size. Click the **Undo** button (the bent arrow icon pointing to the left).

11. Use the **Normal** drop-down menu, which is also in the toolbar.

12. This is the **Format** menu and it applies a set of predefined styles. Select **Heading**, observe the change and, to finish the exercise, click the **Revert to draft** button on the editor header and then click **Close**.

The button **Remove formatting** removes all styles or attributes contained in the text.

Editing a Blogger post (II)

RE-ESTABLISHING A POST AS A DRAFT makes it no longer accessible to others and is saved in the Blogger Drafts file. You can access them and edit them using the available tools whenever you want.

1. When you completed the previous exercise, Blogger's **Stats** tab was probably activated. Click the **Posts** tab in the left-hand panel. ▣

2. The post is now marked as a **draft** ▣. Click on it to return directly to the blog editor.

3. You should now become familiar with the **Editor's** other tools. Next to the **Format** menu you will see the typical text attribute tools: **Bold**, *Italic*, <u>Underline</u>, and ~~Strikethrough~~. Select the first paragraph, eliminate any Bold type by clicking the **B** button and apply italics by clicking the I button. ▣

4. You can also use any of these attribute tools to highlight single words in your text, which will make reading it easier. Do so now by applying bold or italics as you prefer. Remember that, as in any word processor, you must first select the text to change and then press the button. ▣

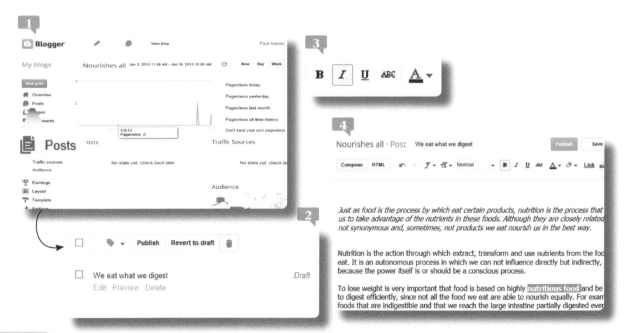

5. You can also highlight text using the following tools: **Text color** and **Text background color**. Each has its own color palette. Select any of the words in bold type, click the **Text Color** button (an underlined T) to display its swatch, and choose the desired color. 5

6. Deselect the text and check that the text has changed to the chosen color. Repeat the process, but do so with a text background color. 6

7. You will use the next block of tools later. Press Ctrl + A to select the whole article and click the **Alignment** drop-down menu which is the first of the next group of tools.

8. Choose the preferred option, but bear in mind that for an article it is preferable to align the text to the left or to justify it (the last button). 7

9. The next two buttons that follow are for creating a numbered or bulleted list, and the next, for creating a quote. 8 Select any of the paragraphs and click it.

10. The alignment and margins change automatically. 9 Finally, click the **Publish** button and cancel the **Share on Google+** box.

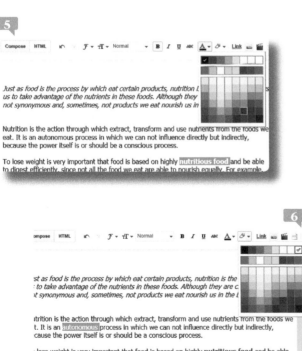

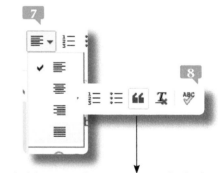

On applying the Quote format, the paragraph style is modified: the margins are increased and it is aligned to the left by default.

Creating a link to a web page

THE BLOGGER TOOLBAR ALSO ALLOWS YOU to create a link on text to another website, another post within the same blog, or even to an e-mail address.

1. For this exercise, download the document, **Digestion begins in the mouth.docx**, from our website and open it. You will be using it shortly.

2. Back in Blogger, place the cursor over the name of the entry that you created in the previous exercise and, of the three options shown, select the **View** option.

3. A new window will open where you will see a preview of the blog post. You may be surprised with how the text looks as it may be different than how it was in the **Editor**, particularly the font and the header. Take note of the differences and, if you wish, make the changes yourself.

4. Leave the window open, but bring the previous one to the foreground, open in the **Posts** tab, and then press **New post**.

Nourishes all · Posts › All (1)

Publish   Revert to draft

We eat what we digest
Edit View Share Delete

My blogs

New post

No matter which Blogger tab is open, the **New post** button is always available.

5. Select and copy the main text of the downloaded document (or another of your choice) and paste it into the text of the post.

6. Do the same with the title of the post.

7. You will now create a link in this post that will take you to the previous post. In the text of the article you will see the words **difficult to digest** in bold type. Select them and click the **Link** button in the toolbar.

8. This opens the **Edit Link** dialog box. In the **Text to display** field, you see the text that was previously selected and the **Web address** option is selected by default. Now, we must copy the address of the previous post into the **Which URL should this link go to?** field. Go back to the window that you had left open in the background, copy your text and then paste it into the aforementioned field.

9. Select the **Open this link in a new window** box so that when the hyperlink is used the linked page does not substitute the open one. Click the **Test this link** button.

10. In this way you can verify that the address indicated is correct. Finally, click the **OK** button.

11. Back in the **Editor**, click the **Save** button to save your changes, place the pointer over the link created, observe the label that appears and go to the next exercise.

IMPORTANT

The **Add 'rell=nofollow'
attribute** option that appears in the Edit link dialog box means that trackers do not take the link into account during their information searches for establishing search rankings. Therefore, it will affect the way that people find your blog.

☐ Add 'rel=nofollow' attribute

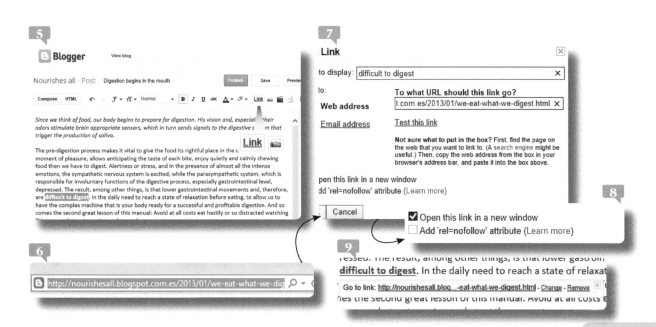

Inserting an image into a post

INSERTING AN IMAGE INTO A POST in a blog is very simple. You can upload it from your computer, choose one that has been previously uploaded to the blog, choose one from your Picasa albums, download it from your mobile, or do it with your webcam.

1. Open the **Digestion Begins in the Mouth.docx** article, in the **Post editor** if you no longer have it open. You will insert an image into this article. Download the **Image 1.jpg** file from our web page and save it on your computer or choose another JPG file of your choice.

2. You will insert an image between the first paragraph (the introduction) and the second. Place the pointer at the end of the first and click **Enter**.

3. Click on the **Insert image** button. It is to the right of the **Link** button. 🗨

4. This opens the **Select a file** dialog box and indicates that the images must be **JPG**, **GIF**, or **PNG** files. You can upload an image from your computer, choose one from the blog, bring it from a Picasa album, mobile, or webcam. Click the **Choose Files** button from the **Upload** option. 🗨

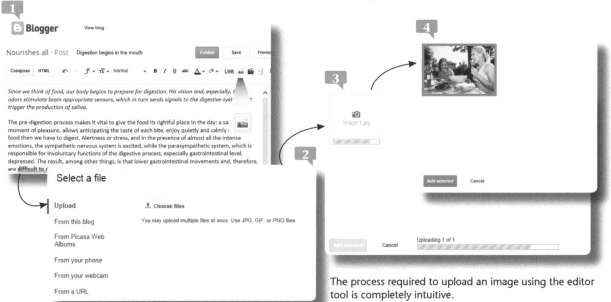

The process required to upload an image using the editor tool is completely intuitive.

5. A dialog box allows you to browse your computer and locate the image. Do so now and click the **Upload** button.

6. You are now back in the **Select a file** box from where the uploading process takes place. ▮3 On completing the process, it will show a thumbnail of the image. You could now easily upload more images, but click the **Add selected** button instead. ▮4

7. The image is added at the place indicated in the text. ▮5 Click the **Preview** button and check the result. ▮6

8. It would probably be best to add a blank line between the image and the text above. Return to **Editor** and do so. Just place the cursor in the right place and press the **Return** key.

9. Now select the image: It shows a floating editing tag that allows you, among other things, to change the size or location of the photo or to add a caption. Select **Add caption**. ▮7

10. Add a line of fictitious text under the image. Enter the text as a caption, ▮8 click the **Publish** button and cancel the box that invites you to share the post.

IMPORTANT

The Google+ application allows mobile phones with Android 2.1 or higher to automatically upload all photos and videos taken with your mobile phone whenever the function is enabled in the application. However, the Google+ application allows you to easily upload photos stored on the phone, one by one.

In this case, the applied options, **Medium** and **Center**, are shown as disabled.

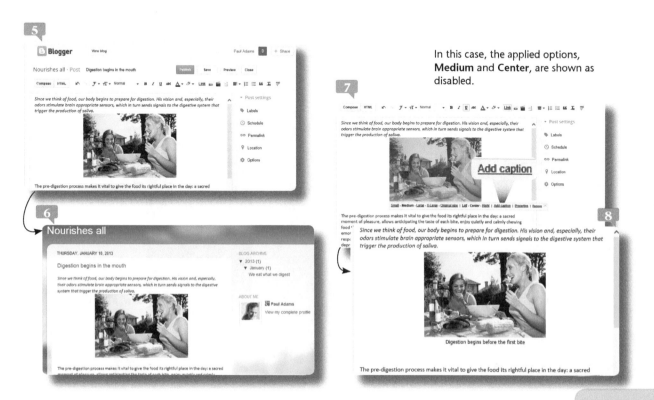

Uploading photographs from your mobile

IMPORTANT

You may need to activate Google+ service location in the **Settings** menu of your mobile phone to be able to use **Instant Upload**.

IF YOU HAVE A MOBILE PHONE with Android 2.1 and iOS 4 or higher, you can upload photos directly from your mobile to Google+, which makes publishing them on Blogger extremely easy. In this exercise you will see how.

1. This lesson is only possible to do if you have a mobile with **Android 2.1** (or higher), or **iOS 4** (or higher). Download the **Google+** application. 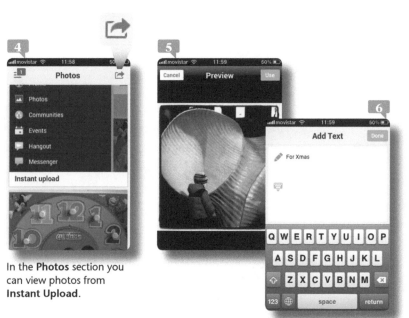 Access it and log in with your Google username and password.

2. You can decide whether or not you want to receive notifications from the application and, on the next screen, search for friends. If you do not wish to do the latter, simply click the **Next** button.

3. The **Instant Upload** service allows you to upload photos and videos to a private album as soon as they are taken by the telephone provided that the application is open (or was recently closed). This makes it very easy to share them with other users of all Google services, including, of course, Blogger. Activate it and take some test shots with your mobile phone camera.

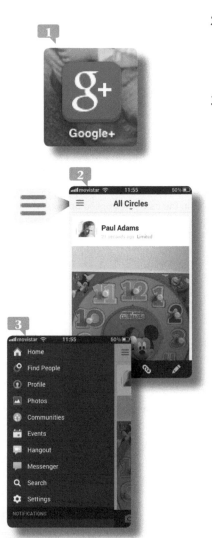

In the **Photos** section you can view photos from **Instant Upload**.

4. From the main Google+ screen on your mobile,  open its menu and select the **Photos** option.

5. Click on the photo icon in the upper right-hand corner of the screen. Find the photo you want to upload on your mobile and click **Use**.

6. A screen opens that allows you to add a comment. Write one and press the **Share** button.

7. The photo is uploaded to the server. On your computer, create a new Blogger post, click the **Insert Image** tool and select the **From Picasa Web Albums** option.

8. You can see the **Photos from posts** album. Click on the picture to open it, select the image, and click the **Add selected** button.

9. Once the image has been inserted, press the **Add selected** button again and choose **From your phone** this time.

10. Thanks to the **Instant Upload** function, images taken with your mobile, since the Google+ application was opened have been automatically loaded. Select one of them and press the **Add selected** button.

11. The image is inserted into the post. Write a title and publish it. Then log into your **Google profile** and see how the picture you published from your mobile looks.

12. Click the **Photos** button, select the **Instant Upload** option.

009

IMPORTANT

The process for uploading videos from a mobile is exactly the same as that described in this exercise.

The **Instant Upload** option allows you to view the private album that is created using the **Instant Upload** feature.

Posting a video from YouTube

POSTING A VIDEO FROM YOUTUBE ALLOWS you to take advantage of the scope of both media in the best way. You do not need to create another account. YouTube is now owned by Google so you can use your Google Account.

1. Without logging out of Google, go to the YouTube site (**www.YouTube.com**).

2. When you create a Google Account, it automatically creates a YouTube channel. You will use it in this exercise. Click the **Upload** link.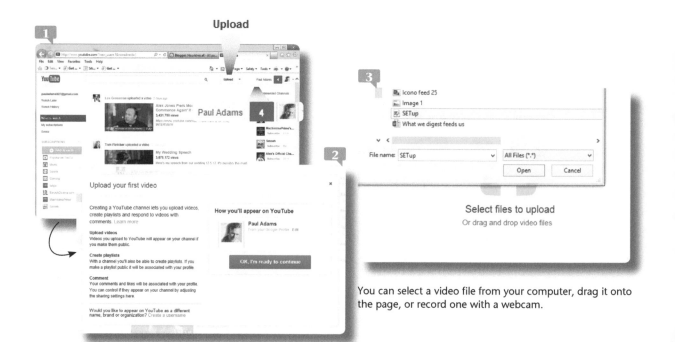

3. If this is the first video uploaded with the active profile, the **Upload your first video** dialog box opens where you can set the type of activities you would like to share on your channel. Do this by selecting the options of your choice and press the **OK, I'm ready to continue** button.

4. As indicated, you can click the **Select files to upload** link, record with your webcam, or drag the file onto the page. Use

You can select a video file from your computer, drag it onto the page, or record one with a webcam.

your preferred method ⬛ or, if you need to, download the **Setup.mov** video from our website.

5. In the **Uploading video** page, insert a title, a description, and relevant tag names. 🔳

6. Open the **Privacy settings** list and select the option of your choice. 🔳 Then select a category and a **License and rights ownership** option.

7. Then, click on the video 🔳 and click on the **Share** option. 🔳

8. Click on the button to the right of the Google+ icon and click on the Blogger icon 🔳 in the menu that appears.

9. A new window opens in which the video has automatically been linked. Type the title and click the **Publish Post** button. 🔳

10. Click the **View blog** button to check the result. 🔳

The **Public** option means that it can be seen by anybody who searches for it, **Unlisted** means that it can be seen only by those people who have the address, and **Private** means that it can only be seen by people who have your permission.

Inserting a video file into a post

YOU CAN ALSO INSERT A VIDEO file directly into a Blogger post. This is done by using the blog editor's Insert a video tool (the clapper boards icon).

1. Go to your Blogger blog's Post editor, place the pointer over the **We eat what we digest** post or another one, if you prefer, and click the **Edit** option. 🔲

2. You will insert a video into this post. Place the cursor somewhere between two appropriate paragraphs and insert a line break, if necessary, using the **Enter** key.

3. Press the **Insert a video** key (the clapper boards icon). 🔲

4. The **Select a file** dialog box opens permitting you to explore your computer to select the video. Click **Choose a video to upload**. 🔲

5. Place the selected file into the window that opens and click the **Open** button.

6. The file name appears in the **Select a file** dialog box. Click the **Upload** button to upload the file. 🔲

7. The box in which the video will be placed will appear in the post and you will be told that the video is being uploaded. Wait for the process to finish.

1

☐ SETup!!!

☐ Xmas

☐ Digestion begins in the mouth

☐ We eat what we digest
Edit | View | Share | Delete

Edit

2

Nourishes all · Post   We eat what we digest   Update   Revert to draft   Preview

Compose   HTML   ↶ ↷   𝓕 ▾ ⫬T ▾ Normal   ▾   B I U ABC A ▾ 🖉 ▾ Link 🔗 🎬 🔲 ▣ ▾ ⋮☰

ingested in large amounts, but in fact there are people who are intolerant of certain products and it is important to be able to identify and eliminate them from your diet. Natural foods usually are not themselves indigestible unless they are ingested in large amounts, but in fact there are people who are intolerant of certain products, and it is important to be able to identify and eliminate them from your diet. the best way is to temporarily removing suspect foods: stop eating them and, if after two or three weeks, digestion is improved, making reinstate test one by one to see which was causing the problem. Proper diet our digestive capacity, balanced and fair is a health guarantee and, therefore, of a weight and body fat indices appropriate. However, when extending digestive problems, intestinal flora deteriorates so that the gut is leaky, ie allows passage to the blood of toxic substances that must be processed in the liver. Eventually the liver suffers from this over-charging and begins to lose efficiency. Gradually
we began
overweig   Upload

            From YouTube

The junk food, My YouTube videos
preservatives,
and fats and   From your phone

            From your webcam

3

Choose a video to upload
By uploading videos, you agree to the Upload Terms and Conditions.

4

Choose a video to upload
By uploading videos, you agree to the Upload Terms and Conditions.
IMG_1398.MOV 0 B / 2.78 MB Remove

Upload   Cancel

Once you have selected the file that you would like to publish, click the **Upload** button in the **Select a file** dialog box.

8. Once the video has been uploaded you will see the first frame in the post. [5] If you do not see it correctly press the **Preview** button. Check the result [6] and indicate whether or not you would like to share the post.

9. Once you have returned to the **blog editor** click on the video box. When the pointer changes into a hand, drag the box and place it at the end of another paragraph.

10. Then, place the pointer on the left of the video box with a click and press the **Insert jump break** button which is to the right of **Insert a video.** [7]

11. A line will be added at the place indicated. To see the effect, press the **Update** button, and then press **View blog** on the Blogger Dashboard.

12. You will see that, although the previous posts are shown complete on the blog's main page, the one that you have just edited is shown only up to the inserted jump break. [8] To see the rest of the post click on the link with the **More information** text that is now below the video box. This will take you directly to a page with the complete post. Any reader who wishes to see the video only needs to press the **Play** button, placed on the box's toolbar, or to click on the center of the video box.

IMPORTANT

You should be aware that Blogger only accepts AVI, MPEG, QuickTime, Real, and Windows Media files. In addition, the files must be no larger than 100 MB.

Jump breaks work very well in long posts as they allow an introductory paragraph of each post to appear on the title page of the blog. This allows the blog to download faster and also improves its position on search engines, which do not like very heavy pages.

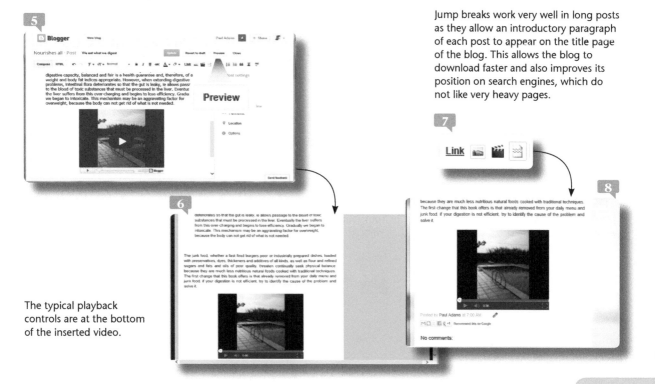

The typical playback controls are at the bottom of the inserted video.

Posting a YouTube video on your blog

IMPORTANT

The **From your webcam** option in the **Select a file** dialog box allows you to make a video with your computer and upload it, all in one spot.

From your webcam

IN THIS EXERCISE YOU WILL SEE that you can insert any YouTube video into your posts regardless of whether it is on your channel or not. You will also see that you do not need to know its address before you do this. The Select a file dialog box allows you to search for a video without leaving Blogger.

1. First, make a video with your mobile phone if you have one that supports the Google+ application (make sure that the Instant Upload function is enabled).

2. Directly in the blog window that you left open in the previous exercise, press the **New post** link. 🔲1

3. Type any paragraph of text, then insert a blank line and click the **Insert a video** button.

4. In the **Select a file** dialog box, press the **From YouTube** option (the second one).

5. You do not even need to know the address of the video that you would like to post on your blog because Blogger allows you to search from this box. Introduce the keywords of a video that you would like to find into the writing field that has appeared. You would like to insert the trailer of a documentary called "Food Inc.," so we write the words **Food Inc**.

1

My blogs

New post

🏠 Overview

📄 Posts

2

Select a file

Upload

YouTube   Food Inc. trailer

From YouTube   Type your search in the box above to find videos.

My YouTube videos

From your phone

From your webcam

The **Insert a video** button allows you to upload a video from your computer, from YouTube, from your mobile, or from your webcam.

3

Food, Inc
ROBERT KENNER FILM
★★★★★ 4 min · Feb 11, 2009

Food, Inc. movie trailer [HD] Official Full Length
Watch this movie free @ free-movie-trial.com A Powerful, powerful documentary that shows us the dark side of food production. Things won't ...
★★★★☆ 3 min · May 14, 2010

Food, Inc. - Too Broke To Eat Well? Junk Food Wins
Watch this movie free @ free-movie-trial.com This is what happens when you are too poor to eat healthy. This family doesn't even realize the ...
6 min · May 14, 2010

TheTruth About Your Food with FOOD, INC. Filmmaker Robert Kenner
twitter.com www.facebook.com www.facebook.com thelip.tv Oscar-nominated director, Robert Kenner joins us to talk about the film and food ...
★★★★★ 56 min · Jul 18, 2012

FOOD INC TEASER TRAILER - "More than a terrific movie -- it's an important movie www.foodincmovie.com In Food, Inc., filmmaker Robert Kenner lifts the veil on our nation's food i

Select   Cancel

and **trailer**. Once we have introduced these keywords click the **Search** button (the magnifying glass icon).

6. Various options that coincide with the search criteria appear. Select one of them.

7. The selected option expands allowing you to preview the chosen video before creating the link. Additionally, you can view a summary of the video, the votin and the overall evaluation. You can now preview any other video from this dialog box. Once you have made your final choice, press the **Select** button.

8. The video is inserted into the indicated place.

9. Give the post a title and click the **Publish** button.

10. Once back in the Blogger Dashboard, click the **New post** button (the pencil icon).

11. In the blank post click on the **Insert video** button.

12. Select the **My YouTube videos** option from the **Select a file** dialog box.

13. This box shows all of the videos that you have uploaded to YouTube with your account. Now click **From your phone**.

14. In this case the videos that you have uploaded with your mobile's Instant Upload function are shown. Click on one of them and then click the **Select** button. Once it has been inserted into the post give it a title and publish it.

Changing date and time, and adding location

THE POST EDITOR CONFIGURATION PANEL ALLOWS you to easily add a location that may refer to the place from where you are writing or any other relevant location. The date of publication can also be modified, and you can even program a future post.

1. Open the blog's first post.

2. You will have notice that once a post has been inserted, its date does not change even though you edit its content. In this exercise you will learn how to modify this using the **blog editor's configuration panel** that is on the right side of the writing area. Click on the section that indicates the date of publication.

3. The box expands and a calendar opens. Select the **Set date and time** option instead of the **Automatic** (the default). You can change the month by clicking on the arrows on either side of the current month. Select a date on the calendar later than today.

4. Click on the field that indicates the time of publication.

5. A list drops down where you can select an option, although you can also introduce a specific time from your keyboard. Set a time with your preferred method.

▼ Post settings

🏷 Labels

🕐 Published on

   1/9/13 7:00 AM
   Pacific Standard Time

🔗 Permalink

📍 Location

⚙ Options

○ Automatic
● Set date and time

Jan 9, 2013   7:00 AM

«   Jan 2013   »
S   M   T   W   T   F   S
30   31   1   2   3   4   5
6   7   8   9   10   11   12
13   14   15   16   17   18   19
20   21   22   23   24   25   26
27   28   29   30   31   1   2
3   4   5   6   7   8   9

○ Automatic
● Set date and time

Jan 15, 2013   7:00 AM

«   Jan 2013   »
S   M   T   W   T   F   S
30   31   1   2   3   4   5
6   7   8   9   10   11   12
13   14   15   16   17   18   19
20   21   22   23   24   25   26
27   28   29   30   31   1   2
3   4   5   6   7   8   9

view   Close

📋▼ ⅈ☰ ☷ 66 𝓘ₓ ✎

▼ Post settings

🏷 Labels

🕐 Published on

   ○ Automatic
   ● Set date and tim

Jan 15, 2013   7:00 AM

12:30 AM
1:00 AM
1:30 AM
2:00 AM
2:30 AM
3:00 AM
3:30 AM
4:00 AM
4:30 AM

6. To save the selected time, click the **Done** button. The time is recorded and as it is a later date than the current time, the post will not be published until the designated time.

7. Sometimes it can also be of interest to give an address in the post. It may be because people often write about places, because you may want to draw attention to your business, or for any other reason. Now you will see how it is done. Click on the **Location** option in the **Post settings** configuration panel.

8. The section drops down and shows a Google map. [5] A message appears asking if you would like to share your location with Blogger.com. Click on the arrow to unfold the options.

9. It can be configured so that the location is shown only in this post or not for this blog. Select the **Always allow** option for this exercise. You can disable it later. [6]

10. In the **Location** panel's search box type an address and click the **Search** button. [7]

11. The address is quickly located and indicated on the map. You can now click **Done**. [8]

12. Click **Update** to publish the post and decide whether you would like to share it with other contacts through another medium.

13. Finally, on the Blogger Dashboard, click the **View blog** button to check the result. [9]

5th Avenue, New York, NY, USA

By default only the address is shown although it is really a link that sends you to a map.

You can search for any direction using the search box in the **Location** option.

Adding tags to posts

ADDING TAGS TO POSTS MAKES THE contents more accessible to users, who can then find entries that are related to topics of interest to them. The Options section also allows you, among other things, to decide whether to allow comments on posts on the entry screen or not. It also allows you to erase comments or to prevent new ones from being added.

1. In the **blog editor**, open the post that you worked with in the previous exercise. You will work with the blog's other **Post settings** options.

2. Click the **Labels** option.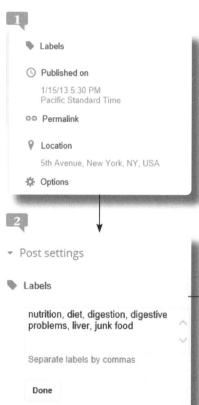

3. To organize posts and to facilitate navigation through the blog, it is advisable to add labels to each post. They should be introduced and separated only with commas. They are normally written in lowercase characters. For your article about nutrition you will use the following tags: nutrition, diet, digestion, digestive problems, liver, junk food. Type the labels that you consider most appropriate.

4. When finished, click **Done** and update the post.

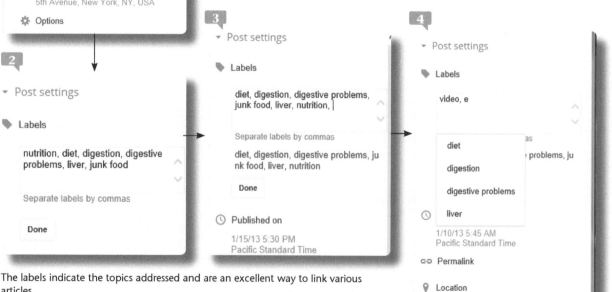

The labels indicate the topics addressed and are an excellent way to link various articles.

5. Open, one by one, the other posts in the editor, assign labels to each of them and update them. Notice that at the foot of the **Labels** section, the terms used are accumulated, [3] and when you begin to write a word, a menu opens with previous labels that start in a similar way. [4]

6. When you have completed the process, you will see that on the Posts page, the labels inserted appear next to each post. [5] Open one of the posts in the **blog editor** to work with the last options in the **Post settings**.

7. Click the **Permalink** option in the Post settings panel. [6]

8. A permanent URL is generated that will allow you to share this post directly as a link on other media and will allow it to be located directly by a search engine. Press the **Done** button. [7]

9. Open the **Options** section.

10. Here you can set whether or not you wish to publish reader comments. If you already have enabled comments on the blog, you can also choose whether to delete all previous comments, or to keep them but not allow new comments. Keep the **Allow** option active, press the **Done** button [8] and, finally, update the post.

IMPORTANT

Each tag generates a URL that will be positioned in Google. It will be more efficient if you frequently add new content associated with the same label. Also, the positioning of the post will benefit from a label that is very similar to its content.

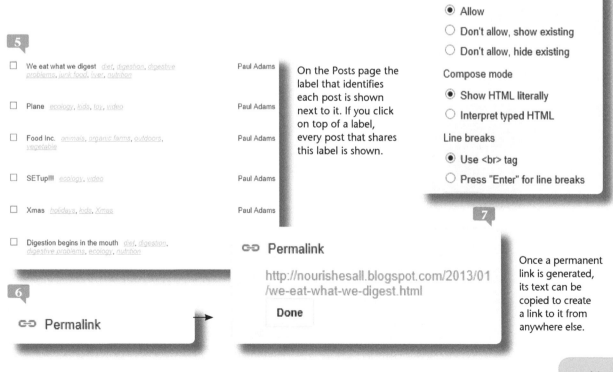

[5]

☐	We eat what we digest *diet, digestion, digestive problems, junk food, liver, nutrition*	Paul Adams
☐	Plane *ecology, kids, toy, video*	Paul Adams
☐	Food Inc. *animals, organic farms, outdoors, vegetable*	Paul Adams
☐	SETup!!! *ecology, video*	Paul Adams
☐	Xmas *holidays, kids, Xmas*	Paul Adams
☐	Digestion begins in the mouth *diet, digestion, digestive problems, ecology, nutrition*	

On the Posts page the label that identifies each post is shown next to it. If you click on top of a label, every post that shares this label is shown.

[6]

Ⓖ Permalink

[7]

Ⓖ Permalink

http://nourishesall.blogspot.com/2013/01/we-eat-what-we-digest.html

Done

Once a permanent link is generated, its text can be copied to create a link to it from anywhere else.

[8]

⚙ Options

Reader comments

- ◉ Allow
- ○ Don't allow, show existing
- ○ Don't allow, hide existing

Compose mode

- ◉ Show HTML literally
- ○ Interpret typed HTML

Line breaks

- ◉ Use <br> tag
- ○ Press "Enter" for line breaks

Creating a label list

TO MAKE THE LABELS REALLY USEFUL, create a label menu in the blog. Blogger allows the labels to be presented in the form of either a drop-down menu or a cloud.

IMPORTANT

The interesting thing about labels lists is that each label represents a link that allows all posts that refer to it to be shown with a single click.

1. On the **Blogger Dashboard** click on **View blog**.

2. At the foot of each post is a list of all its labels. 🗨 Go back to the previous page.

3. You will now place all the labels in the sidebar in such a way that allows users to surf via the posts that are linked to them. Click the **Layout** option to open its page. 🗨

4. Later on you will work with this window in detail, but for the moment, click on **Add a Gadget** in a location that appears appropriate for the page. 🗨

5. A new window opens from which you can choose the gadget that you wish to add. Use the scroll bar to find the one called **Labels** and click the **Plus** button (+). 🗨

2

New post

- 🏠 Overview
- 📑 Posts
- 📄 Pages
- 💬 Comments
- Google+
- 📊 Stats
- 🏆 Earnings
- 📊 Layout
- 📌 Template
- 🔧 Settings

3

Add a Gadget

4

Labels
Show all the labels of posts in your blog.
By Blogger

1

Posted by Paul Adams at 5:15 AM   No comments:
Recommend this on Google
Labels: animals, organic farms, outdoors, vegetable

Labels:

5

Configure Labels

Title	Labels
Show	○ All Labels ⦿ Selected Labels Selected labels: 16 of 16 edit
Sorting	⦿ Alphabetically ○ By Frequency
Display	⦿ List ○ Cloud
	☑ Show number of posts per label

Save   Cancel   Back

6. In the **Configure Labels** window, you can set a different title such as **Topics** or **What we mean.** You can also choose whether to display all labels or only some of them. Select the **Selected Labels** option and click the **edit** link.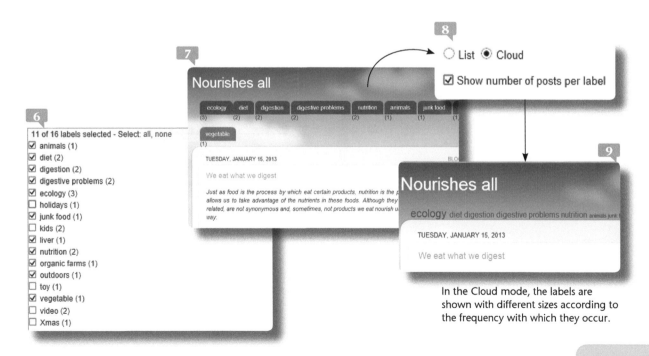

7. A panel appears at the bottom of the window where you can deselect any of the labels created. Do so now if you wish and press the **Done** link to return to the previous window.

8. Labels can be displayed alphabetically or by frequency, in which case the most frequently repeated labels in the blog will be shown first. Choose the **By frequency** option.

9. They can also be displayed either as a **List** or as a **Cloud.** Keep the first option selected and you will soon see the difference.

10. Keep the **Show number of posts per label** option active, click the **Save** button and then click **View Blog.**

11. You can now see, at the top of the page, the list of labels that are organized in order of frequency and indicate the number of posts. Ctlick the navigator's **Back** button and, in the **Layout** panel, click the **Edit the created gadget** link.

12. In the **Labels** option panel select **Cloud.** Deselect **the Show number of posts per label** option and click **Save.**

13. View the blog again to check the result.

In the Cloud mode, the labels are shown with different sizes according to the frequency with which they occur.

Checking and configuring your blog stats

THE BLOG STATS PAGE SHOWS THE number of visits your blog has received in a very graphic and understandable way and also allows you to choose what time frame to analyze.

1. Click the **Stats** tag on the **Blogger Dashboard**. 🔲

2. This page shows the visit statistics for your blog. They will not be significant right now, although the idea is to get them to rise gradually. 🔲 First, you have a graph showing the number of visits per day obtained during the last week. If you pass the pointer over it, a floating label indicates the values corresponding to each point on the graph. 🔲

3. On the right you will see the number of page views today, yesterday, in the last month, and since the creation of the blog. Click the **Don't track your own pageviews** link. 🔲

4. In the dialog box that opens, select the **Don't track my pageviews** option to prevent your own visits, which are of no interest, from being counted. Click the **Save** button. 🔲

Stats

Pageviews last month   24

Pageviews all time history   24

Don't track your own pageviews

1/10/13
Pageviews: 2

1:8:13   1/10/13

Pageviews

Pageviews y

Pageviews l

Don't track your own pageviews

You can tell Blogger not to include your own pageviews in its stats. To do this, Blogger must add a blocking cookie to your browser. If you use more than one browser, open each one and set this preference.

○ Track my pageviews
● Don't track my pageviews

Your current browser is MSIE 10.0

Save

016

5. For this option to work, just as it indicates, the browser must permit cookies. Open the **Privacy** tab in the browser's **Options** dialog box.

6. Note that activating the option does not modify the previous visit count. It will work only for future visits. Below the graph you will see the number of visits for each blog post. Simply clicking the name of any of them will open a new window. Click the **More** link (to the right of the title of this section).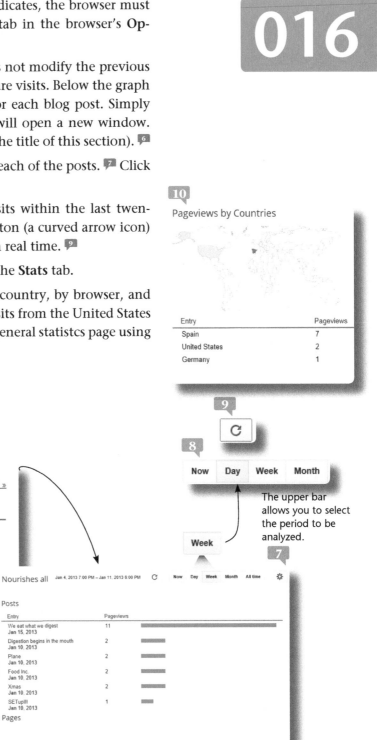

7. A bar graph appears for the visits to each of the posts. Click the **Day** button in the header.

8. The graph changes to show the visits within the last twenty-four hours. The **Refresh stats** button (a curved arrow icon) allows you to refresh the statistics in real time.

9. Now press the **Audience** button in the **Stats** tab.

10. The number of visits are shown by country, by browser, and by operating system. In your case visits from the United States dominate. You can return to the general statistcs page using the **Overview** link.

10

Pageviews by Countries

Entry	Pageviews
Spain	7
United States	2
Germany	1

9

C

8

Now	Day	Week	Month

The upper bar allows you to select the period to be analyzed.

Week

7

6

Posts   More »

Entry	Pageviews
We eat what we digest Jan 15, 2013	11
Digestion begins in the mouth Jan 10, 2013	2
Plane Jan 10, 2013	2
Food Inc. Jan 10, 2013	2
Xmas Jan 10, 2013	2

Nourishes all   Jan 4, 2013 7:00 PM – Jan 11, 2013 6:00 PM   C   Now Day Week Month All time   ⚙

Posts

Entry	Pageviews
We eat what we digest Jan 15, 2013	11
Digestion begins in the mouth Jan 10, 2013	2
Plane Jan 10, 2013	2
Food Inc. Jan 10, 2013	2
Xmas Jan 10, 2013	2
SETup!!! Jan 10, 2013	1

Pages

No stats yet, check back later.

Applying a Blogger dynamic view

IMPORTANT

Google presented the dynamic templates in April 2011. Although at that time it supported neither gadgets nor customization, it has gradually allowed the blog owner some control as was promised.

THE DYNAMIC TEMPLATES ARE SEVEN HIGHLY visual views that display spectacular effects when moving from a post or a page to another. They allow users to choose which of the seven views they would like to use, as well as to share or follow the information with one click.

1. Activate the **Template** tab on your blog desktop. 🔲

2. It is best make a security copy of the blog to ensure that you can restore its former appearance at any time. This is especially important when the blog has many previously incorporated customizations, although this is not the case now. Click **Backup / Restore**. 🔲

3. This opens a dialog box of the same name. Click the **Download full template** button. 🔲

4. Select the **Save** option to save the XML file on your computer and close the dialog box.

5. The seven Blogger dynamic templates are shown. Place the pointer over the first dynamic view. Of the two options that appear, select **Customize**. 🔲

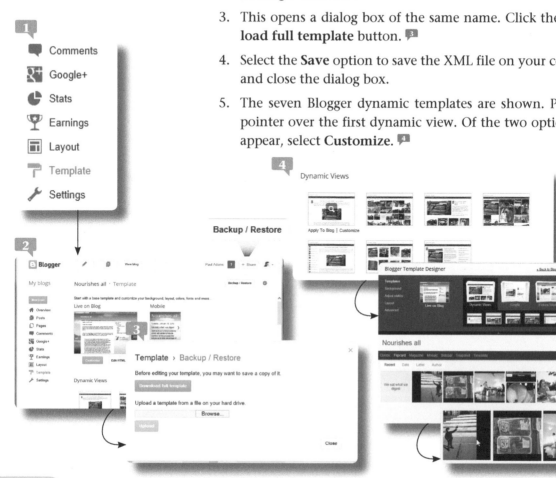

46

6. The **Blogger Template Designer** opens. At the top, the different categories of templates are shown and, in the second row, the templates available for the chosen option (in this case dynamic views). Click on the second view and see how the blog is updated.

7. This is the **Flipcard** view. It shows the images of the blog as a background. **5** If you place the pointer over one of the images the image turns. **6** If you click on the image, the post opens in a new window. **7** Do so now and then close the window. In the blog preview click on the **Flipcard** tab.

8. The selected view is the one presented by default, but the user who accesses the blog can switch between them using the dropdown menu. In the **Blogger Template Designer**, choose the fifth dynamic template.

9. This is the so called **Sidebar**, which allows you to navigate using the Posts bar on the left. **8** Choose the sixth customized view.

10. In the **Snapshot** view entries are organized as a board of photographs. **9** Continue experimenting and finally apply the fourth template called **Mosaic**. **10**

11. In the **Mosaic** template, the blog's images and text are of varying sizes in a freely composed mosaic that changes whenever the blog is updated. Click on one of the posts to open it. **11**

IMPORTANT

In the dynamic views, buttons are automatically incorporated at the bottom of each post allowing you to share them on Google+, Twitter, and Facebook.

  +1 0   Tweet 0   Like 0

If you need to interrupt your work before moving on to the next lesson or at any other time, click the **Apply to blog** button in the **Template Designer** header. If your connection is slow, do so after applying any changes to make sure they are not lost.

The dynamic views allow the user to switch freely between them.

Modifying dynamic templates

ALTHOUGH INITIALLY DYNAMIC TEMPLATES SUPPORTED NEITHER gadgets nor customization, Google introduced these features in 2011 and, among other things, made it possible to change the background, colors, and fonts in the blog.

1. In Blogger Template Designer click the **Background** tab. **1**

2. You can change the template's color scheme of the template. Try one of the suggested colors. **2**

3. Click on the arrowhead in the miniature **Background image**. **3**

4. You can choose any option from the extensive image gallery that Blogger offers classified into categories or upload a photo from your computer. Click the **Upload image** tab. **4**

5. Locate an image on your computer that is less than 300K or, if you prefer, download the image from our website called **Sunflower background.jpg** and use it. Once it has been uploaded, press the **Done** button. **5**

6. The image is applied to the background. Open the menu that shows the selected **Tile** option. You can choose whether or

Templates

Background

Adjust widths

Layout

Advanced

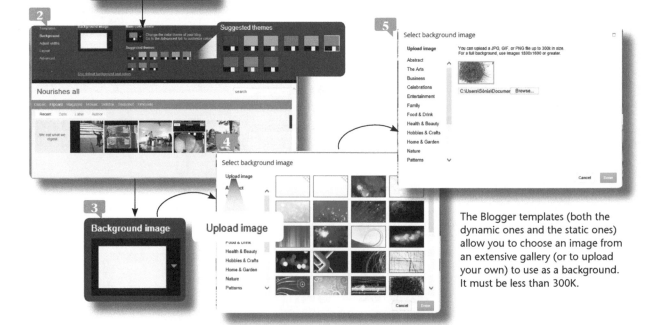

The Blogger templates (both the dynamic ones and the static ones) allow you to choose an image from an extensive gallery (or to upload your own) to use as a background. It must be less than 300K.

not the picture should be repeated to fill the background and in what fashion. You can also decide if it should move with the page or not and how it should be aligned.  Now click the Template Designer's **Advanced** tab.

7. Keep the **Page** category selected in the second panel and choose a font for the post's text.

8. The **Header** category in the second panel refers to the title's Background bar, but as we are using a photograph we cannot modify it. The **Header Bar** category modifies the blog's Menu Bar and allows you to change the background color, the font, and the color of the text. Make changes as you please.

9. In the section called **Links** you can establish a change in color of the links when the pointer is placed over them, as well as if they have been already visited by the user. Activate this panel and modify the default colors.

10. You can change the title's color and the font. Select this option and choose one that contrasts with the background.

11. Open the **Post Title** section, make your modifications. Then click **Apply to blog** and **View blog**.

IMPORTANT

In the **Advanced** tab of the Template Designer, the **Date** ribbon section allows you to modify the stamp that indicates the date of each post. If you wish to eliminate them from the whole blog, use the following code in the **Add CSS: ribbon {display:none !important;}** section.

If you click on a color sample of one of the selectors, a panel unfolds that allows you to create your own color or to set transparencies.

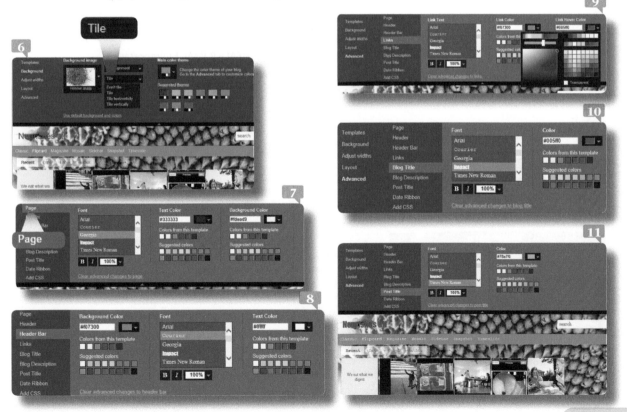

Modifying the CSS code of a dynamic template

BLOGGER ALSO ALLOWS CUSTOMIZATIONS OF DYNAMIC templates using CSS code from the Blogger Template Designer. In this exercise you will use this feature to create a customized header for your blog.

1. For this exercise you can download the file called **Header.jpg** from our website or create your own header. Our image measures 110 x 182 pixels and has a resolution of 72 dpi.

2. In the **Template editor**, in the **Background** tab, click the **Remove image** link in the **Background image** section.

3. In the **Advanced** section, select the **Add CSS** option.

4. In this panel you can add customized codes. You will add a code that will insert a customized header. Write the following code, or download it and copy the archive **Header code** that you will find on our website:

```
.header-bar {
background-color:#536fa8 !important; /*t background-color*/
background-image:url(URL HEADER IMAGE) !important;
background-repeat:no-repeat;
height:148px !important; /* Header height */
```

The value **!important** makes the style overwrite that of the template.

Once a background image has been inserted, it can be deleted at any time.

The loaded image can be found in the **Album** file of the **Photos** section.

border-bottom:20px solid #f07300; /* Border bottom */

}

#header .header-bar .title h1, #header .header-bar .title h3 {display:none;}

#header a:hover {text-decoration:none !important;}

#main {margin-top:125px !important;} /* Distance between the header and content */

5. In a new window, log in to your **Google** profile, click on the **Photos** tab, 🔲 and then click the **Upload new photos** button. 🔲

6. Load the header image using whichever method you prefer and click on **Create album**. 🔲

7. When loaded, press the **Cancel** button in the **Share** box.

8. Select the **Photos** option from the sidebar 🔲 and click the **Albums** option 🔲 from the header. Access the photo, right-click your mouse and select the option **Copy**. 🔲

9. Return to the **Template Designer** and in the code that was created substitute **URL HEADER IMAGE** with the location of the image that you have just copied.

10. You should then be able to see the change in the Preview part of the screen. If not, click the **Apply to blog** button and then the **View blog** link to see the result. 🔲

IMPORTANT

The code that we present in this exercise allows you to modify the height of the header and the footer, and the distance between the header and the content (indicated in pixels). You can also modify the color of the background as well as that of the footer, whose codes are preceded by a numeric sign (#).

Once a photo has been placed in an album, it will have a URL that can be used for other purposes.

We have used the sky blue from the image (**#536fa8**) as the background color of the header.

Retrieving a template and editing a static template

IF YOU CHOOSE ONE OF BLOGGER'S static templates you will lose dynamism but will gain considerably in control. To begin with, both the advanced options as well as the number of available templates are considerably increased.

1. From your blog's **Dashboard** go to the **Template** section.

2. You must recuperate the original template. Click the **Backup / Restore** button.

3. Click the **Browse** button in the window that appears, locate the backup copy that you created a few exercises ago, and click **Open**.

4. Click **Upload** from the dialog box. Check in the **Live on Blog** thumbnail that the original theme with its gadget has been applied again to the blog.

5. Place the pointer over a template that is not dynamic and click the **Customize** link.

6. As with the dynamic views, this takes you to the **Blogger Template Designer**. Change the background as you wish.

7. Go to the **Layout section.**

In this example you have used one of Blogger's backgrounds. Blogger's static templates do not have the spectacular effects of the dynamic views, but they do offer a greater degree of control and freedom to the user. They also allow you to use more gadgets.

8. There are various designs for both the blog as well as for the pages. They can be applied by clicking on one of the themes. In the preview area you can see the design applied to the blog and can modify it. Click the header's **Edit** link. 5

9. This dialog box allow you to change the text and description of the blog. It also allows you to load an image for the header from your computer or a URL. Furthermore, you can specify if you will substitute this text and what its relative placement will be. Add a description 6 and change the header, if you wish. Click **Save**.

10. Choose a template that you like and activate the **Advanced** section.

11. You have more options than with the dynamic templates with the advantage that on selecting one of them, the element in question is surrounded by a dotted line. Some, however, refer to items that are not yet in the blog. Make your changes to the color and the font. Then click the **Apply to blog** button.

12. Click the arrowhead on the bar that separates the **Designer** from the preview area. 7

13. The Designer hides itself allowing a complete view of the blog. 8 Open the **Designer** again and click **Back to Blogger**.

IMPORTANT

When the blog template is modified, the template for mobiles is also automatically modified. If you would like to make changes to the template for mobiles independently, click the icon below the thumbnail. You can choose a different template for mobiles.

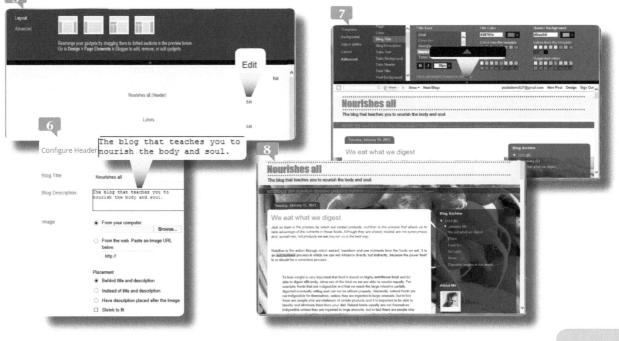

Configuring comments

BLOGGER ALLOWS YOU TO MANAGE YOUR comments: You can decide if your blog supports comments from all or from only certain registered users, how they are displayed, and whether they require moderation, among other aspects.

1. For this exercise, it would be ideal if you could get some comments on your blog (if you do not already have any). Share it with friends and ask them to leave an opinion. By default, Blogger will only publish comments from users that have accounts with Google, LiveJournal, TypePad, AIM, or OpenID.

2. Enter your Blogger Dashboard, open the **Settings** menu and select the **Posts and Comments** option.

3. Here you can define certain criteria for these two elements. If you click the **Add** link in the **Post Template** field, a box opens that allows you to introduce a code that will be applied whenever a post is written. The **Showcase images with Lightbox** option disables the function that expands an image in a pop-up window.

Stats
Earnings
Layout
Template
Settings
　Basic
　Posts and comments
　Mobile and email
　Language and formatting
　Search preferences
　Other

Nourishes all · Settings › Posts and comments

Posts

Show at most ?　　7　posts ▾ on the main page

Post Template ?　　Add

Showcase images with Lightbox ?　　Yes ▾
　　Yes
　　No

Comments

Comment Location ?　　Embedded ▾

Comments

Comment Location ?　　Embedded ▾

As there is an increasing number of spam comments, Blogger allows you to control who can comment on your blog.

Who can comment?
　● Anyone - includes Anonymous Users
　○ Registered User - includes OpenID
　○ User with Google Accounts
　○ Only members of this blog

Comment Moderation ?
　● Always
　○ Sometimes
　○ Never

Comment Form Message
　Tell us what you think...

　Remove

4. With regard to comments, you can configure them to be displayed below each post and on the same page (the default option), to be displayed in a pop-up window or as a full page, to hide them. Select your prefered option. ▣

5. You can also determine the type of users who are permitted to comment on your blog. Select the **Anyone** option (albeit provisionally). ▣

6. In the **Comment Moderation** field, choose the **Always** option so that each comment can be reviewed before its publication. ▣ Keep the **Yes** options selected in the **Show word verification** field and **Hide** in the **Show Backlinks** field.

7. You can also add a message for the comments field. Do so now ▣ and press **Save settings** and then **View blog**.

8. Click on the link to comment on one of your posts, ▣ introduce comments, ▣ and publish it.

9. Your signature appears automatically. ▣ Click the **Sign out** link in the page's header. ▣

10. For the moment you are not the author of the blog. Go to the next exercise without signing into Blogger.

In the next exercise you will see what one of your blog's readers will encounter when trying to make a comment, among other things.

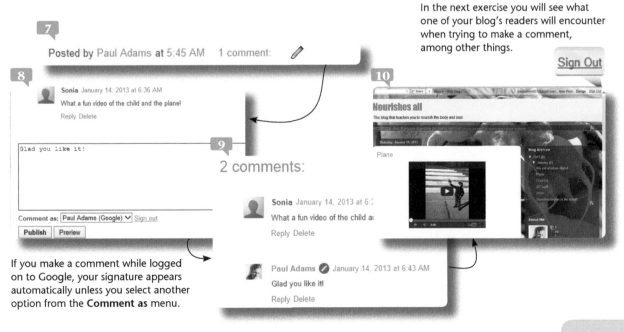

If you make a comment while logged on to Google, your signature appears automatically unless you select another option from the **Comment as** menu.

Managing comments

IMPORTANT

Responding to comments on your blog is as important as writing posts (as is commenting on the blogs of others). However, many users make comments to market themselves, insult, or provoke. Erase immediately any comment with insulting or violent content, as well as those spam comments that only seek to generate visits to another site or sales. Ignore provocative and empty comments and, above all, never lose control of your blog.

ONCE COMMENTS HAVE BEEN MADE ON your blog, you can manage them as you wish. You can remove their content retaining the signature of the author together with a notification of the action, you can completely erase it or mark it as spam, among other things.

1. Without signing in to your Google Account, enter a new comment in a blog post, but this time select the drop-down menu in the **Comment as** menu and choose the **Anonymous** option. **1**

2. Through the **Show word verification** option, you are asked to type some verification letters. Do so now. **2**

3. As you had previously activated the **Comment moderation** option, you are informed that the comment will not be published immediately. **3**

4. Introduce an anonymous comment that includes the URL of another page but select the **Name/URL** option from the **Publish as** menu. Introduce any signature **4** and complete the publication.

1

Comment as: | Select profile...
Publish | Google Account
 | LiveJournal
 | WordPress
 | TypePad
 | AIM
 | OpenID
 | Name/URL
 | Anonymous

2

Please prove you're not a robot

163 alibloy

Type the two words:

163 alibloy

3

Publish

Your comment will be visible after approval.

4

Edit profile ×

Name:
Sonia Llena ×

URL:

Continue

5

Nonsense...

Comment as: Saboteur () Edit

Publish Preview

6

New post

🏠 Overview
📋 Posts
📄 Pages
💬 Comments
    Published
    Awaiting moderation
    Spam

Google+
Stats
Earnings

5. Enter one last comment and, this time, sign as **Saboteur**. 5

6. Next, log into your Blogger account again, then go to your blog's Dashboard and finally to the **Comments** tab. 6

7. In the **Published** section, in this case, are those that were published before the blog's settings were changed and the one that you wrote yourself a moment ago. You can see the names of the authors on the far right. 7 Now click the **Awaiting moderation** tab.

8. You would not want to publish the comments of a user that signs as **Saboteur**, would you? Place the pointer over this one and click the **Spam** option. 8

9. Display the options for the two remaining comments, but choose the one called **Publish**.

10. Select the **Spam** tab and note the post options.

11. The **Not spam** option publishes it immediately. Select this option. 9

12. Open the **Published** tab, place the pointer over the comment by **Saboteur** and click the **Remove content** option. 10

13. You can select various comments at a time and apply any of the following actions, **Remove content**, **Delete**, and **Spam**, which are also in the header. 11 Select the name of the post that contains **Saboteur**'s comment, see how it looks. 12 Check that the other comments also appear correctly.

IMPORTANT

If the **Hide** option is selected from the **Show backlinks** command (as in your case), no link will be created to any URL that has been included in a comment.

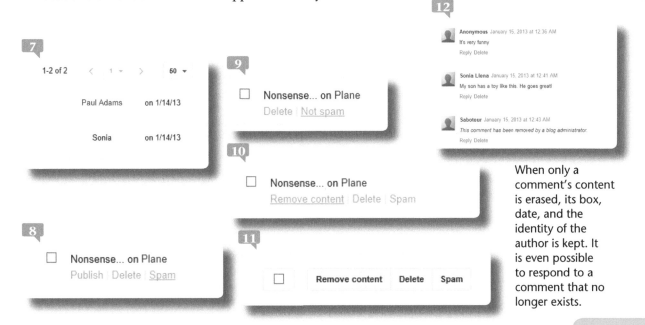

When only a comment's content is erased, its box, date, and the identity of the author is kept. It is even possible to respond to a comment that no longer exists.

Adding pages to your Blogger blog

BLOGGER PAGES ARE ACCESSIBLE from anywhere in the blog with one click. It is advisable to include pages with information about the page itself, its authors, contact information, site policies, or conditions, although you can create pages with any content.

1. Click the **Pages** tab on your blog **Dashboard**.

2. At the moment you only have the main page. 🔲 Click **New page** and select the **Blank page** option. 🔲

3. The **Page editor** opens where you can create any type of content. In this case you will create a page about the author. Create a title and a short biographical paragraph, and add a photo, just as you would in a post. 🔲

4. We will share a little trick with you: Go to the web page **www.foxyform.com** and fill in the simple form that you will find there. 🔲

5. When you click the **Create formular** button, you will be given an HTML code that defines a contact form. When you have done this, copy the code that has been generated 🔲 and return to the Blogger **Page editor**.

6. Click the HTML tag that will show the code for your page, press the **Enter** key at the end of the last line of the code and paste here the copied code.

7. Go back to the **Compose** view and check the result.

8. Thanks to this form you don't need to publish your e-mail address, which would make you an easy target for spam. This also generally increases the number of messages as the process is easier for the users. Open the **Page settings** section and erase the comments.

9. Make sure that you have given the page a title and click the **Publish** button.

10. In Blogger's **Pages** section you can see the page that you have created. Create a third test page with any content.

11. Use the **Show pages as** drop-down menu, select the **Top tabs** option and click the **Save arrangement** button. Then click **View blog** to check the result.

12. You will see a new band with three tabs. Select one of them to see the result.

13. Return to Blogger and change the **Show pages as Top tabs** option for the **Side links** option. Save the changes and check the result again. Select the option that you prefer.

IMPORTANT

If you click on the Edit link (below the name of the main page in the Pages section), a pop-up window appears with which you can change the name of the page.

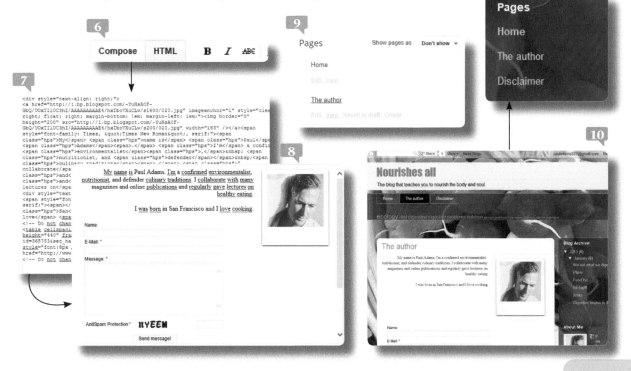

Controlling your blog feeds

FEEDS ALLOW YOUR READERS TO RECEIVE updates of your blog on a different site, (a feed aggregator), that collects the contents of all the blogs followed. This makes it easy to track your blog.

1. Click Blogger's **View blog** button and go to the end of your blog.

2. You will find the **Subscribe to: Posts (Atom)** link. By clicking on the link the user can access a page from which the subscription can be configured. Do so and click on **Subscribe to this feed** for demonstration purposes.

3. In the dialog box, keep the defaults and click **Subscribe**.

4. Go back to the **Dashboard**.

There are two commonly used standards for feeds: RSS and Atom.

5. You will now see how to add a feed icon to your template next to the link to give it more visibility. Go to your blog's **Template Designer**.

6. Select the **Advanced** tab and click the **Add CSS** option and introduce the following code:

Blogger blogs have a default feed. You can also view your blog's default feed by going to the following URL: http://NAME OF BLOG. blogspot.com/feeds/posts/default.

```
.feed-links {
padding-right: 280px;
padding-top: 3px;
background: url(URL-DEL-ICONO) center left no-repeat;
}
```

7. The second and third lines show the location of the link. The URL address indicates where the icon is located. You can download from our website the one that we have used as an example (**icon feeds 25**). Test the effect, publish the blog, and return to Blogger.

8. Click the **Settings** tag and unfold the **Other** category.

9. The first section precisely controls the site's feeds. In the **Allow Blog Feed** menu, the **Full** option distributes all of the content of the posts. You can also distribute them just up to the jump break or up to the first characters (approximately 400) using the **Short** option. Select your preferred option.

10. You can also add a footer that will appear at the end of each post feed. Click the **Add** link and add some text in the text box that appears (if you think it could be of some use).

11. Finally, click the **Save settings** link.

> **IMPORTANT**
>
> Your readers can also subscribe to your blog directly from their feed aggregators by introducing your site's URL. Including a link for this makes the process easier.

4

Blogger Template Designer   « Back to Bl

Templates	Sidebar Background	Add custom CSS Learn more about editing template code
Background	Images	Add CSS here to override existing styles...
Adjust widths	Feed	
Layout	Feed Links	
Advanced	Pager	
	Footer	
	Mobile Button Color	
	Add CSS	

Q Share   1   More ▾ Next Blog»   pauladams927(

Nourishes all
The blog that teaches you to nourish the body and soul.

5

You've never lost the desire to eat for a thrill? Faced with excessive stimulation to the sympathetic system (either for joy or a deep depression, daily stress or the impact of an image on the TV) can lose their appetite completely forget lunchtime, suffering a indigestion or simply digest more slowly than usual, feeling of heaviness that means. Ah, we caution from now: **do not think that by skipping a meal will lose weight. To lose weight the first thing you need is to acquire good habits and healthy, and regularity is one of them.**

Posted by Paul Adams at 2:21 AM   No comments:

Recommend this on Google

Labels: diet, digestion, digestive problems, ecology, nutrition

Home

6

Site feed

Allow Blog Feed ?   Full ▾

Post Feed Redirect URL ?   Full

Post Feed Footer ?   Until Jump Break

Enable Title Links and Enclosure   Short
Links ?
                     None
OpenID
                     Custom

You can determine the amount of information included in your feeds.

You can allow links to be created to the multimedia files included in your posts.

7

Allow Blog Feed ?   Until Jump Break ▾

Post Feed Redirect URL ?   Add

Post Feed Footer ?   See you soon!

                     Remove

Activating FeedBurner as a feed manager

A FEED MANAGER OFFERS YOU TOOLS for controlling the distribution of your feed among your subscribers. Google's feed manager is called FeedBurner, and one of its features is access to interesting statistics. To use it you must sign up for FeedBurner.

1. Go to **http://feedburner.google.com**. Insert your blog's address and click Next. 🗨

2. Select a feed associated with your account (you can choose between Atom or use RSS). Click **Next**. 🗨

3. The name given to the feed and its address is indicated. Take note of it and change it if you wish. Click **Next**. 🗨

4. A new feed has been created. 🗨 Click **Next**.

5. FeedBurner will create reports of how many people have subscribed to your feed, which feed readers they use, and which other services they receive. You can also find out how often they access your blog via other links, how many elements were download, the popularity of specific elements in your

1

Looking for feeds you used to have at feedburner.com?

Claim your feeds now »

– OR –

Burn a feed right this instant. Type your blog or feed address here:

http://nourishesall.blogspot.com   ×   ☐ I am a podcaster! Next »

2

Identify Feed Source

The feed URL you entered is:

http://nourishesall.blogspot.com

FeedBurner discovered more than one feed at that address. Please select one to use as your source:

○ Nourishes all - Atom: http://nourishesall.blogspot.com/feeds/posts/default
● Nourishes all - RSS: http://nourishesall.blogspot.com/feeds/posts/default?alt=rss

Next »

3

Give your feed its title and feedburner.com address:

Feed Title: Nourishes all

Enter a title to help identify your new feed in your account.

http://feeds.feedburner.com/
Feed Address: NourishesAll

The address above is where people can find your new feed.

Next »   Cancel and do not activate

4

🔥 FeedBurner™

1. Claim your feed	2. Enhance Your Stats

Congrats! Your FeedBurner feed is now live. Want to dress it up a little?

Subscribe to your feed (and share with others!) at:

blog, as well as the number of people who have visited or clicked on information in your blog. Select the options that you want **5** and click **Next**.

6. Acces your FeedBurner feed. In the **Analyze** tab your blog's statistics are shown divided into the categories you have chosen. As information is still to be compiled, it will be blank. **6** The **Optimize** tab offers various ways of optimizing your feed, **Publicize** offers tools for increasing the number of followers, **Monetize** allows you to add third-party advertisers to your feeds, and **Troubleshootize** offers solutions for the most common problems.

7. In another window, open the **Others** tab from the Blogger's **Settings** section. In the field called **Post Feed Redirect URL** add the URL that FeedBurner gave you a few steps ago. **7**

8. Save the configuration.

9. If you enter your original feed **8** you will be automatically redirected to FeedBurner's feed. **9** Try it out.

Once you have created your feed in FeedBurner and it has been linked to your blog, anyone who accesses your blog's feed will be redirected to the new feed.

Adding more relevant gadgets to the blog

IN THIS EXERCISE WE WILL ADD some of what we consider to be Blogger's most relevant gadgets. Each one has a settings box that allows its name to be customized.

1. This exercise is dedicated to inserting gadgets. Click the **Layout** tab on your blog's Dashboard.

2. Click on one of the **Add a Gadget** links.

3. Select the **Follow by Email** gadget.

4. Substitute the message for one that invites your readers to subscribe to the e-mail service and click **Save**.

5. The text will be added to the blog next to a field in which readers can subscribe by inserting their e-mail address. You can select the gadget that was created and place it where you wish. Now add the **Subscription Links** gadget after customizing the title. This is a gadget that allows you to choose which feed aggregators your readers can use to read your blog. It also permits users to subscribe to comments and posts separately.

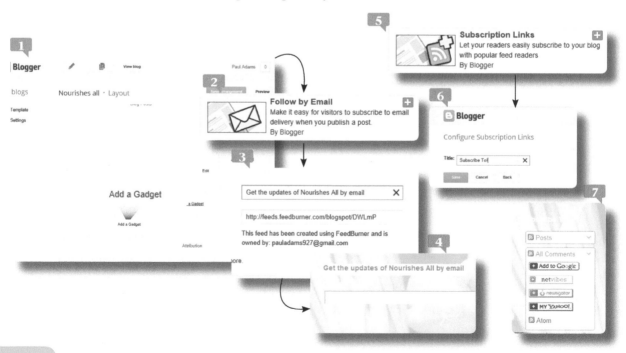

6. Insert the **Link List** gadget ⁸ As you will see you can add URL addresses and names for the sites. Introduce a few and click the **Save** button. ⁹

7. A list of names will be created with links to their respective sites under the specified title and in the place indicated. ¹⁰ Add the **Followers** gadget ¹¹ and, in its configuration box, personalize the name and deselect the **Use template default styles** option.

8. You can now personalize it. Do so now, if you wish, and click **Save.** ¹² The profile photos and names of the blog's followers will be shown.

9. If you do not wish to add any other gadgets, check and correct the organization of your page if necessary.

10. Click the **Edit** link in the **Favicon** field. ¹³

11. A favicon is a favorite icon that appears in specific places in your blog. It should be treated as an archive with an .ico format. It can be created on many sites (we have used **www.favicon.cc.** ¹⁴ Download it in the **Configure Favicon** window and remember that it will not appear immediately in your blog. ¹⁵

12. Check the result with a preview. Click the buttons **Save arrangements** and **View blog** to check the appearance and the functionality of the added gadgets.

IMPORTANT

The term favicon comes from "favorite icons". It is the icon that identifies your blog in a list of markers or favorites, in a tab, or in your navigator's history list. It makes your site more immediately identifiable. To avoid having to load it, each time it is saved in your computer's cache. You will probably need to erase cache and cookies to be able to see changes in the favicon.

Publishing without Blogger

IMPORTANT

In the Mobile and e-mail section in Blogger's Settings tab you can configure the publication of posts from your mobile. Click the **Add mobile** link in the Mobile section, send the code that appears to go@blogger.com, and follow the instructions. The messages will be charged at your mobile provider's usual rate.

THE BLOGGER APPLICATION FOR MOBILES ALLOWS you to publish posts with images and videos from your mobile phone. With Blog This! you can do so directly from your browser's Menu Bar without needing to enter Blogger's website.

1. On your mobile phone, download the **Blogger** application by Google.

2. When you have installed it, open it, read and accept the terms of service conditions,  and tap the **Sign in** button.

3. Allow Blogger to access your computer and to use your current location. Choose an option from the **Select Location** menu, press **Done**, and then press **New Post**.

4. You will see a Post editor that allows you to create new posts at any time.  Type a title in the **Post title** field and text in the **Post content** field  and press the keyboard icon to hide the keyboard.

5. Insert label text in the **Label** field and then press the camera icon.  Take a photo and press **Use**. Repeat this to add more photos.

Insert a couple of blank lines below the text to separate the image from the text.

The photograph icon (to the right of the camera icon) allows you to upload photos stored in your mobile.

6. Make a long key press on one of the added images, select the **Remove** option 8 to erase it, and, finally, press **Publish** in this window and then in the next.

7. All of the blog posts are shown. The posts can be edited or erased by pressing the arrowhead button to the right of each of them. 9 The blog's mobile version can be seen if you press the **View** option. 10

8. On your computer, go to Blogger's Help center: **http://support.google.com/blogger/** and in the search field type **Blog This!** and press the **Enter** key. 11

9. Go to the **What is Blog this!?** link and drag the link 12 to your browser's link bar 13. If you cannot see it, you should first activate it by going to the menu in the browser's header.

10. Click on the button that has just been created and enter a new post in **Blog This!** without having to go to your page in Blogger. 14 It has almost all of Blogger's editing tools, and by accessing the menu in the upper left-hand corner you can choose in which blog you would like to publish the post (if you have more than one). Complete the process and publish the post. Then click **View blog.**

IMPORTANT

You can create an e-mail address that publishes each received message as a post. Write some secret words in the empty field in the **Publish posts via email** section (the Settings tab, Mobiles and e-mail section, Email subsection Save the setting). Any messages sent to the address indicated will be either published or sent to the Drafts folder, depending on the option you have established.

You can also edit a blog by pressing on its title. The button on the lower right-hand corner allows you to switch to another one of your blogs, among other things.

BlogThis! <-- drag this link to your browser's Links bar

A small icon indicates where the Blog This! button has been placed.

Inviting new authors and administrators

YOU MAY WANT YOUR BLOG TO have various authors or even administrators with full editing rights. It is extremely easy to set up and manage.

1. Go to the **Basic** tab in the **Settings** section. 🔲

2. You will work in the **Permissions** section. Click the **Add authors** link 🔲 and click the button **Choose from contacts**. 🔲

3. Enter the e-mail addresses of the authors you would like to invite to share the blog and when finished click **Invite authors**. 🔲

4. You will be told that the invitations are pending. 🔲 Each of the authors will receive an e-mail with a link. If they click on the link and start a session with a valid account, they will be able to create their own posts, which will appear in **Settings** in the **Blog authors** section next to your name, maintaining a different status: that of **Administrator**. 🔲

1

- Pages
- Comments
- Google+
- Stats
- Earnings
- Layout
- Template
- Settings
  - Basic
  - Posts and comments
  - Mobile and email
  - Language and formatting

2

| Paul Adams | pauladams927@gmail.com |

+ Add authors

3

| Paul Adams | pauladams927@gmail.com | Admin |

+ Add authors

Invite authors   Choose from Contacts   Cancel

Anybody Edit

4

| Paul Adams | pauladams927@gmail.com | Admin |

+ Add authors

abcgdra@gmail.com
slleandabd@gmail.com
nsakdhewiuha@gmail.com
ansjk647@gmail.com

Invite authors
Invite authors   Choose from Contacts   Cancel

Anybody Edit

When you click on a contact it will be added to the list at the bottom of the dialog box.

5

▸ 3 open invitations.

You can enter the e-mail addresses of the invited authors one by one or select them from your contact list.

5. If you click the arrowhead button in the **Author** box, you can change the status from **Author** to **Admin**. ▼ While an author can write, edit, or erase their own posts, an administrator has access to all of the blog's configuration, design, and template options. The administrator can erase the posts of any author. ▣

6. Should you wish to erase an author, you need only click on the X link on the right-hand side and confirm that you wish to cancel the author's access to the blog. The author will no longer be authorized to create new posts, although previous posts will remain published.

7. Below each post is the author's name and a link to his or her Blogger profile (if it is public). ▣ Try it.

8. You can also decide who may access the blog's content through the **Permissions** form in the **Basic** section under the **Settings** tab. By default, Blogger's blogs are open to all readers who access the site, but you can decide to restrict access to the site's authors or to a specific list of readers that you can create by introducing their e-mail addresses or by importing their addresses from your contact list. Finish this exercise by saving the blog's configuration and by encouraging your authors (if you have any) to start writing!

IMPORTANT

Remember that you can invite as many people as you wish to become an author or an administrator of your blog.

All of the authors and administrators invited to your blog will be able to access it from their Blogger Dashboard. Their available options will depend on their status.

Below each post appears the name of each author and the date and time of its publication. There will be a link to the author's profile if it is public.

Creating a blog and profile in WordPress.com

WORDPRESS.COM IS THE OTHER IMPORTANT FREE service that allows you to create a blog with an acceptable level of customization, free hosting, and the possibility of contracting additional fee-paying services.

1. Start with a new blog. Go to **www.wordpress.com** and click **Get Started.**

2. Fill in the form. You should choose an e-mail address, a blog address, and a username that are not already in use as well as a secure password. Its security level will be shown on the right. When you have completed the form click **Create blog** to access the free version.

3. At the address you gave, you will receive an email that will allow you to start work. When you have received it click **Activate Blog.**

4. You can choose a theme among the hundred or so offered by the service. When you have chosen one, click on its thumbnail.

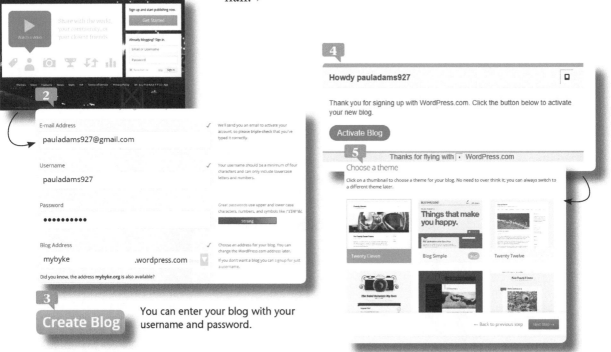

You can enter your blog with your username and password.

5. Before finally applying a theme, you are shown a large preview, a description of the theme, and a list of elements that allow for editing (these vary depending on the theme). You can apply the theme by clicking the **Next Step** button or go back by clicking **Back to previous step**. Now choose a theme. 6

6. WordPress informs you that the theme is being activated and shows the **My Blog** page. On this page you could start a new blog by clicking **Create a new blog**, but click the **Settings** button instead. 7

7. Click the **Public Profile** tab and fill in the form for your public profile on WordPress.com. 8 Click the **Change your Gravatar** link to choose a profile image.

8. A window opens telling you that you can upload an image from your computer, take a photo with your camera, supply a URL, or use a WordPress.com pre-made gravatar. Choose the first option. You need not worry about the size of the file, nor do you need to trim the image.

9. Select the image and click **Next**. In the next window adjust the image and click the **Crop and Finish!** button. 9

10. Give the image a classification; G means that it is suitable for all viewers and X means that it contains scenes of violence or explicit sex. Click on the image, select the **Confirm** option and go back to WordPress.com to save the changes.

IMPORTANT

A gravatar is an image that identifies you globally, together with your signature, in blogs and other sites. It is related to your e-mail address. When you create a WordPress.com profile, an associated gravatar profile is automatically generated.

Crop your photo using the dotted box below

Publishing a page on WordPress.com

IMPORTANT

On the WordPress.com Dashboard **Right Now** indicates the current content of your blog. For the moment, they have all been added by WordPress.com. The **QuickPress** panel introduces the contents of a blog directly from the Dashboard. The next sections allow you to see and manage comments, drafts, and statistics. The last one offers the latest news as well as the blogs and posts featured on WordPress.com.

AS IN BLOGGER, WORDPRESS.COM ALLOWS YOU to create pages and posts. In this exercise you will create a presentation page for your project or business to get to know the WordPress.com page editor.

1. Go to WordPress.com and click the **My Blog** tab. Then click on the name of the blog created.

2. You will see a preview of an almost empty blog. We say *almost* because it contains one model blog and one page, both of which were created by the application. Click on your blog's name in the left-hand corner of the header to show the menu. Select **Dashboard**.

3. As in **Blogger**, from the WordPress.com Dashboard you can create and manage posts, comments, and pages; change your blog's settings; and much more. This is done using the tabs panel on the left or the options in the center. Click on the **Pages** tab and select **Add New**.

The WordPress Dashboard offers some interesting tools at a click.

4. The **Add New Page** screen opens. As you already know how to, insert a title and text that defines your project. Then click the **Add Media** button 5 that you can find in the top left-hand corner of the toolbar (the icon is a camera on top of a musical note).

5. Upload an image from your computer by dragging it to the center of the **Insert Media** window and clicking on the **Select files** button.

6. Once the image has been loaded, complete the form that appears. 6 You will see that you can decide whether the image should remain at the bottom of the text or if it should be aligned in another way. You will also be able to change its size and edit its URL. When you have finished, click the **Insert into page** button.

7. The image is inserted at the position of the cursor. In the **Publish** panel click **Preview,** 7 go back to the **Editor** and make the necessary changes. Click **Publish** to check the result. 8

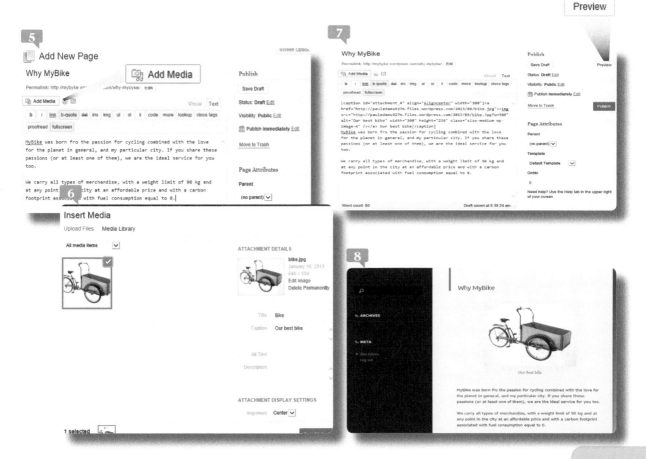

Creating and erasing a post in WordPress.com

THE POST EDITOR IN WORDPRESS.COM IS almost identical to the one you saw earlier for editing pages. It is even easier than the Post editor in Blogger. Remember that the posts are what give your site the character of a blog. They appear in succession and are organized in chronological and (normally) reverse order.

1. Click the **Posts** tab on the panel to the left and select the **Add New** option.

2. Insert a title, text, and a relevant image following the same steps as in the previous exercise. Click **Add Media**.

3. The image is inserted into the place indicated. Click on the text in the caption and note that it can be edited.

4. Click on the **Text** tab in the **Editor** to access its code and go back to the **Visual** tab.

5. Check the URL given to the post, click **Edit** and then OK if you decide to change it.

6. In the **Categories** section, click **Add New Category**, insert a name and click **Add New Category**.

When the Dashboard's side tabs are selected the options are shown.

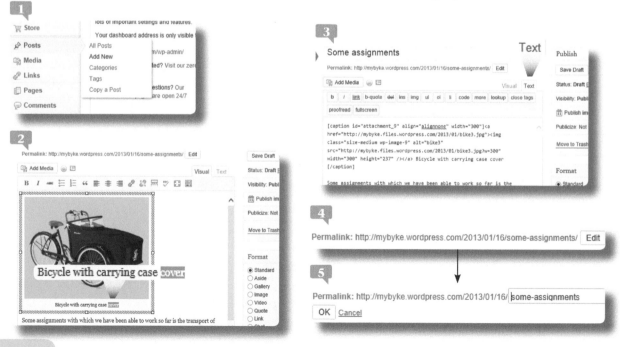

74

031

7. Blogger also allows you to insert labels. Do so now in the correct section remembering to separate the names with commas. When you have finished click **Add**. Once the tags have been inserted, any one of them can be eliminated by clicking the icon to its right.

8. Publish the post and check the preview. The panel on the left, as well as encouraging you to write more posts, suggests additional tags based on the information on the image and the post. Click on those you would like to add and see how this happens.

9. Close the panel on the left by clicking on the cross, and open the blog by clicking on its name on the far left of the header.

10. Before the new post just created, you will see the test post. In the blog's header you can see the page you created as well as the page called About (created by Blogger by default). Return to the **Dashboard**, click on the **Posts** tab and select the **All Posts** option.

11. Place the pointer over the welcome post from WordPress.com and erase it by selecting **Trash**.

12. Place the pointer over the post that you created, select **Edit** and go to the next exercise.

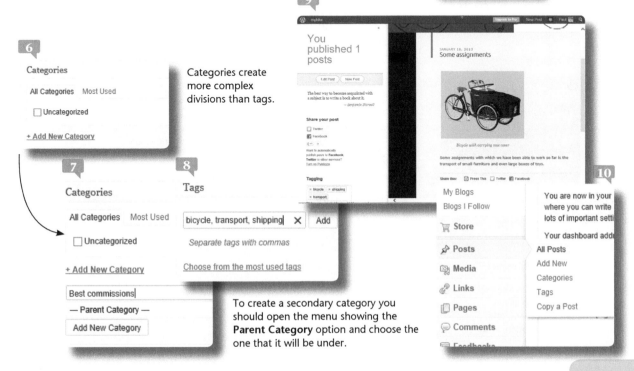

Categories create more complex divisions than tags.

Separate tags with commas

Choose from the most used tags

To create a secondary category you should open the menu showing the **Parent Category** option and choose the one that it will be under.

Editing an image and inserting a link

AFTER INSERTING AN IMAGE INTO A post or a page, it can be edited to modify its link, give it a border, or to customize its position. A More tag can be inserted into the text to divide it or a link to other pages can be added.

1. You can edit an image that is already inserted into a post or page. Click on the image in the post you have opened from the previous exercise and then on the photo icon. 🔲

2. Using the **Edit Image** control box you can reduce the size of the image, change its alignment, or correct the text. You can also remove all links using the **None** option or modify or recuperate a link (if it has been erased) with **Current Link**.

3. Click on the **Advanced Settings** tab. 🔲

4. You can modify the size of the image, edit it with a CSS code, and give it a border. You can also modify the vertical or horizontal space. Type the number **3** into the **Border** field and a number **10** into the **Vertical Space** field. Check the result in the preview 🔲 and click **Update**.

5. Correct the post's text and type a couple of sentences above the image and a couple below it. Place the cursor at the end of

The **Edit Image** tab allows the image's alignment, title, alternative title, caption, and URL to be modified.

The **Advanced Settings** tab allows you to apply a border and to modify the location of the image using numeric values.

the photo's caption and click the **Insert More Tag** icon (two rectangles separated by a broken line).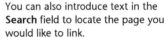

6. A break and a link something like "**more**" will be inserted so that only the first part of the post will be shown on the title page. Depending on the template applied, it may or may not have an effect. Apply bold type, italic, or attributes wherever you wish and then select a place in the text to create the link.

7. Click the **Insert/edit link** button (an unbroken chain link) and in the window that opens click **Or link to existing content**.

8. Select one of the pages that were already created for the link or insert the URL of a site you would like to link. Then click **Add Link**.

9. The hyperlink is shown underlined. It also has the same quotation mark button for creating quotes. Click the tool on the far right.

10. Another toolbar opens. It contains a text formatting menu, some additional styles (text color, underline, and justified alignment), options for copying unformatted text or text in Word format, for removing formatting, for inserting special characters, for modifying margins, for undoing and redoing commands. Click **Update**.

You can also introduce text in the **Search** field to locate the page you would like to link.

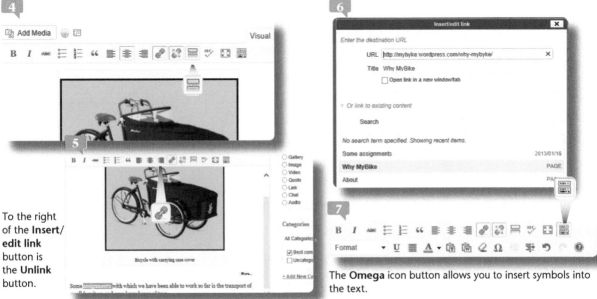

To the right of the **Insert/edit link** button is the **Unlink** button.

The **Omega** icon button allows you to insert symbols into the text.

Using QuickPress and aligning an image

THE QUICKPRESS FUNCTION ALLOWS YOU TO create posts and even insert images from your blog's Dashboard. In this exercise you will see how this is done as well as how to limit a text to one side of an image.

1. Click the **Dashboard** tab and in the **QuickPress** module insert a title and some text for a new post. Click **Add Media**. 🔲

2. Load the image and complete the form. 🔲 Then click **Insert into post**.

3. You are sent back to your **Dashboard** and as the post was written in the **QuickPress** module, you cannot see the image. 🔲 Insert names for the tags 🔲 and click **Publish**. When you are told that the publication has been made, click the **View post** link. 🔲

4. You can see the post. 🔲 Return to the Dashboard and, in the **Your Stuff** module, click the **Edit** link of the post you have just created. 🔲

1

For a future on two wheels   ×

📷 Add Media ⊕ ▤

As QuickPress does not give access to the editing options that you have seen previously, one alternative would be to use QuickPress to write the post, save it as a draft, and then access it later with the Editor.

2

ATTACHMENT DETAILS

bike2.jpg
January 16, 2013
500 × 307
Edit Image
Delete Permanently

Title   bike2

Caption   Bike ride

Alt Text

Description   All our bikes have been purchased to move and transport.

ATTACHMENT DISPLAY SETTINGS

3

Right Now

Content		Discussion	
1 Post		1 Comment	
2 Pages		0 Approved	
2 Categories		1 Pending	
5 Tags		0 Spam	

Theme Dusk To Dawn with 0 Widgets

Akismet blocks spam from getting to your blog. There's nothing in your spam queue at the moment.

QuickPress

Have you tried our new home page quick post form yet? Try it now →

For a future on two wheels

📷 Add Media ⊕ ▤

src="http://mybyke.files.wordpress.com/2013/01/bike2.jpg?w=300" alt="Bike ride" width="300" height="184" class="size-medium wp-image-16" /></a> Bike ride[/caption]

Tags: Separate with commas

Save Draft   Reset   Publish

4

bike, children, move, utopia

Remember not to repeat synonyms in the tags.

5

Post published. View post | Edit post

5. Place the cursor at the place in the post you would like the image to appear (after adding any necessary jump breaks) and click **Add Media**.

6. Click the **Media Library** tab. 8

7. You will find the images that you uploaded a moment ago. Click on the thumbnail of the image you would like to insert.

8. Select the **Full size** option and then click **Insert into post**.

9. Click on the inserted image and then click **Align left**. 9

10. The image is aligned to the desired side and the text sticks to it. Select the text that remains on top of the image and stick all of the text to the right of the image.

11. Click on the image again and when the transformation lines appear, pull the lower right-hand corner to adjust it to fit the text.

12. Select the text and click **Increase left margin** until you like the way it looks. Click **Preview** to check the result 10 and, finally, update your post.

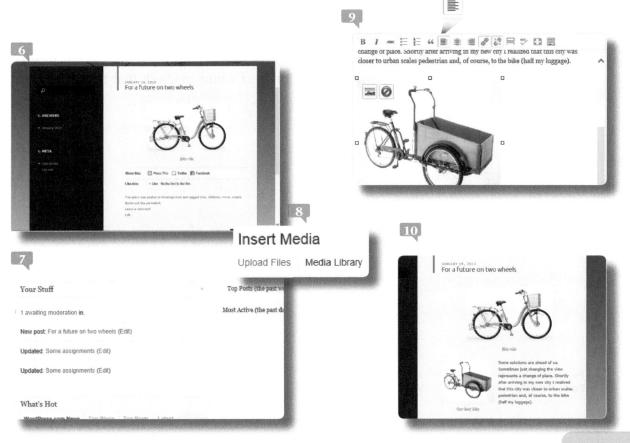

Copying text from another word processor

IMPORTANT

If you deactivate the **Keep linebreaks** option in the **Paste as Plain Text** dialog box, the text will be copied as a single paragraph.

COPYING TEXT DIRECTLY FROM ANOTHER WORD processor, such as Word, may generate a code that is very complicated and prone to errors. In this exercise you will learn how to avoid this using the correct tools. You will also look at other advanced editing tools.

1. Select the **Add new page** option from your blog's menu, the header or the **Pages** tab on the **Dashboard**.

2. For this exercise you will copy Word text. If you do not have a document you can use, make one now. Make sure that it includes text styles paragraph formatting.

3. Select and copy the text and return to WordPress.com. Unfold the full toolbar using the **Show/Hide Kitchen Sink** button and click the **Paste as Plain Text** button.

4. A new window opens. Press **Ctrl + V** to paste the text into it and click **Insert**.

5. The text is pasted without the text and paragraph formatting. Open the text editor to check that the HTML code

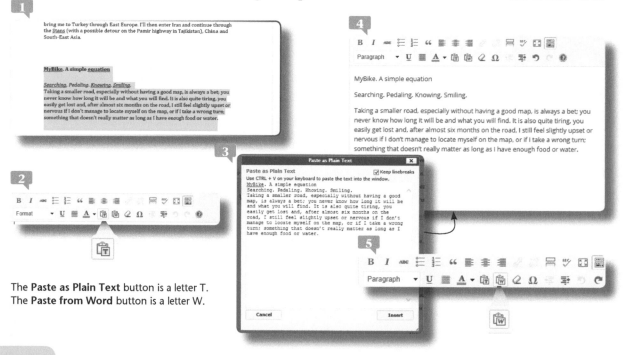

The **Paste as Plain Text** button is a letter T.
The **Paste from Word** button is a letter W.

does not contain any additional information. Return to the **Visual Editor** and click **Undo**.

6. Now click the **Paste from Word** button.

7. In the box that opens press **Ctrl + V** to paste the contents of the clipboard.

8. You can see that the text maintains the original appearance. Click **Insert**.

9. The result is as expected. Make any necessary corrections, apply styles if you wish, and click the **Distraction Free Writing** button (the second to last button in the first row of tools).

10. A view opens that allows you **to just write** and offers only the essential text editing tools. Click the **Exit fullscreen** link.

11. Click **Remove formatting** and note how the text styles are removed but the paragraph styles are not.

12. Click **Undo**, if you wish, followed by the **Insert Custom Character** button. Pass the pointer over them and note how the corresponding HTML code is shown. Click one of them to insert it into the text and then click **Undo**.

13. Insert an image and publish the page.

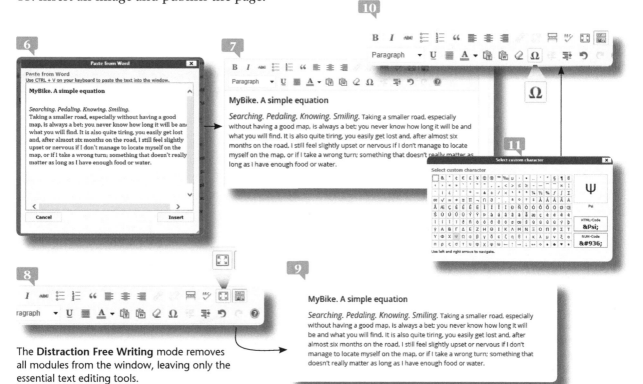

7

MyBike. A simple equation

Searching. Pedaling. Knowing. Smiling. Taking a smaller road, especially without having a good map, is always a bet; you never know how long it will be and what you will find. It is also quite tiring, you easily get lost and, after almost six months on the road, I still feel slightly upset or nervous if I don't manage to locate myself on the map, or if I take a wrong turn; something that doesn't really matter as long as I have enough food or water.

6

Paste from Word

Paste from Word
Use CTRL + V on your keyboard to paste the text into the window.

MyBike. A simple equation

Searching. Pedaling. Knowing. Smiling.
Taking a smaller road, especially without having a good map, is always a bet; you never know how long it will be and what you will find. It is also quite tiring, you easily get lost and, after almost six months on the road, I still feel slightly upset or nervous if I don't manage to locate myself on the map, or if I take a wrong turn; something that doesn't really matter as long as I have enough food or water.

Cancel   Insert

The **Distraction Free Writing** mode removes all modules from the window, leaving only the essential text editing tools.

9

MyBike. A simple equation

Searching. Pedaling. Knowing. Smiling. Taking a smaller road, especially without having a good map, is always a bet; you never know how long it will be and what you will find. It is also quite tiring, you easily get lost and, after almost six months on the road, I still feel slightly upset or nervous if I don't manage to locate myself on the map, or if I take a wrong turn; something that doesn't really matter as long as I have enough food or water.

Page styles and copying a page

PAGES ON LOWER LEVELS ARE DISPLAYED in an unfolding menu when their principal page is clicked. The Copy page option allows new pages to be created using styles applied to a previous page.

1. We will continue to work with the page created for the previous exercise, so either keep it open in the **Editor** or open it again if you closed it.

2. Make any necessary adjustments and in the **Page Attributes** module, unfold the menu called **Parent** ▮ and select the **About** option. ▮

3. Unfold the **Template** menu and select a variation of the applied template (if you have one). In our case we will remove the right sidebar.

4. In the **Order** field you can configure a particular order for the page instead of the chronological order that is applied by default. Do so if you wish ▮ and click the **Update** option in the **Publish** module.

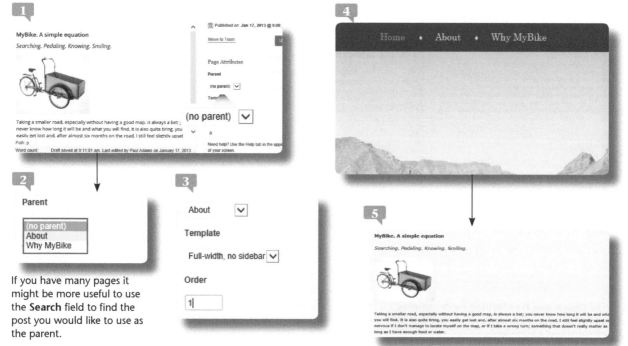

If you have many pages it might be more useful to use the **Search** field to find the post you would like to use as the parent.

82

5. Access your blog from its title in the header and place the pointer over the **About** tab.

6. You will see the title of the page that was made. Select it and check that the template has been modified.

7. Unfold the blog's menu and select **Page** from the **New** option.

8. In the **Writing Helper** click the **Copy a Page** link.

9. Select the recently created page and click **Copy**.

10. The previous page is pasted into the one that has just been created, while maintaining the styles. Change the title, substitute the text for another from a page suited to this style, select the image, and click **Add media**.

11. Insert a new image and modify its size, if necessary, and deactivate the **Show likes** option in the **Likes and Shares** module, so that the **Like** box is not displayed at the bottom of the post.

12. Publish the post and click the **View Page** link in the header of the editor.

13. Check the result and unfold the **About** page menu.

IMPORTANT

If you are writing a post you will find the **Copy an article** function in the Writing Helper. It allows you to use a previously created post as a template. The **Copy a Page** and **Copy a Post** options can also be found in menus within the **Pages** and **Post** tabs in the sidebar.

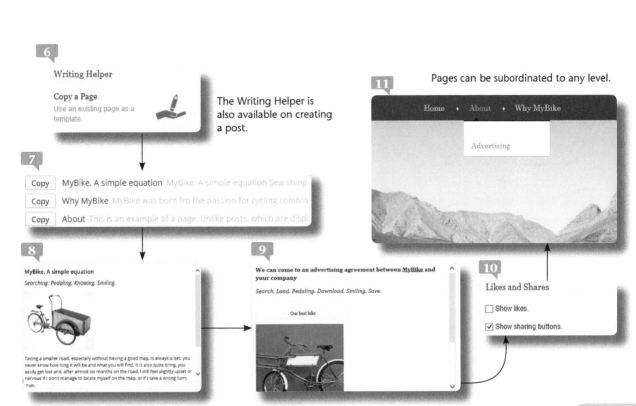

The Writing Helper is also available on creating a post.

Pages can be subordinated to any level.

Asking for an opinion before publishing

THE WRITING HELPER ALSO ALLOWS YOU to send an e-mail to a contact, directly from WordPress.com, requesting an opinion about a post or a page before publication. The contact will receive an e-mail with links to a preview that contains a field into which the contact can write comments.

1. Create a complete post.

2. Suppose that you have written a post and you would like to ask a friend's opinion about it before you publish it. In this exercise you will see how to do so without having to use your e-mail or leaving WordPress.com. Click the **Request Feedback** link in the **Writing Helper** module. 🔲

3. The module expands and you will see a field in which you should introduce the e-mail addresses of the people from whom you would like feedback. Do so now and click the **Customize the message** link. 🔲

4. A new field opens where you will see a draft of the message created by WordPress.com by default. Do not erase the message

Path: p
Word count: 92
Draft saved at 9:56:51 am.

Categories
All Categories   Most Used
☐ Best commissions
☐ Uncategorized
+ Add New Category

Writing Helper

Copy a Post
Use an existing post as a template

Request Feedback
Get feedback on this draft before publishing.

Likes and Shares

Request Feedback

Get feedback on this draft before publishing.

Writing Helper

[Back] Request Feedback

Get feedback on this draft before publishing.
Enter email addresses of people you would like to get feedback from:

dsajkkd@gmail.com, scdewi@gmail.com

[Send Requests]   Customize the message to dsajkkd@gmail.com and 1 more

Get a share link without sending an email.

Hi,
I started writing a new draft titled "Do you know the world could be better on a bike?" and would love to get your feedback. I plan on publishing it shortly.

Please leave your feedback here:
[feedback-link]

Title:
Beginning: Everybody needs some time to think. When everything around you is hectic and busy, there's

Send Requests

[Send Requests] Cancel

between the square brackets [feedback link]. This is the link that the recipients will use to reply to the message. When you have edited the message, click **Send Requests**.

5. The module is updated and you are informed that the responses will be shown in this very module. Save the post as a draft.

6. In the image you can see the appearance of the message that your friends will receive. Upon clicking one of the links in the message, a preview of the post opens with a panel on the right where comments on the post can be introduced. When they have finished, they only need to click the **Send Feedback** button to send their feedback.

7. You will receive it on your WordPress.com site. To read it, open the draft created and open the **Writing Helper** module again.

8. You will see a green icon for those who have sent a reply and a red one for those who have not. If a comment if preceded by a plus sign (+) it means that the message is only partially shown. Click on the icon to expand the full message.

IMPORTANT

Below your friends' feedback you will see two links. **Link** displays the preview that was sent to them and **Revoke access** revokes their privileged access.

4

Back | Request Feedback

Requests sent.

When your friends read your draft and give feedback, you'll get an email and the feedback will appear below.

Send more requests.

You can send as many feedback requests as you please.

5

Hi,

I started writing a new draft titled "Do you know the world could be better on a bike?" and would love to get your feedback. I plan on publishing it shortly.

Please leave your feedback here:
http://pauladams927m.wordpress.com/?p=22&shareadraft=522cb788bec6f

Title:
Beginning: Everybody needs some time to think. When everything around you is hectic and busy, there's nothing like a bike ride to give you some 'me time'. . . . Whether you're on the way to work, riding for leisure or just trying to get a break from the kids, the world looks better from the saddle. It's a cheap...

Read more: http://pauladams927m.wordpress.com/?p=22&shareadraft=522cb788bec6f

Thanks,
Paul Adams

6

mybike | ✔ Following | ★ Like

Paul Adams would like your feedback.

This is a private, unpublished draft. Please review it and leave your feedback in the box below.

Note any typos you find, suggestions you have, or links to recommend.

The people from whom you have asked for feedback can see a preview version of your post or page.

7

Send Requests | Customize the message

Get a share link without sending an email.

xxxxxx6@gmail.com

January 17, 2013 | Link | Revoke Access

Yehuda Moon is a genius! Blog and strips are fantastic!!!!

Modifying screen options

IMPORTANT

Excerpts can appear in the feeds as well as on the title page of the blog, in search results, or in the author's files, manuals, or categories. In any case, it will always refer to the subject covered.

THE SCREEN OPTIONS PANEL IS COMPRESSED in the header of the Posts screen. It allows some modules, such as Extract and Comments, that are hidden by default to appear. You will look at these in this exercise.

1. Click the **Screen options** button just under the header on the far right of the editing screen of the last post created. [1]

2. A panel opens in the upper part of the screen. All available module options for the **Editor** are displayed in the **Show on screen** section. Right now, only those modules whose boxes are ticked are shown. Select **Excerpt**, **Discussion**, **Author**, and Revisions [2] and click the panel again to compress it.

3. You will see that many new modules have appeared. In the **Excerpt** module [3] introduce an excerpt from the page that describes the post in just a few words. [4]

4. Click **Publish** and open the blog from the link in the header.

If neither an excerpt nor a More tag has been inserted, the title page of your blog will display the first 55 characters of each post by default.

5. To start with, the post's default 55 character-long excerpt can now be seen on the title page. This is of great importance as it will help the readers to access the information they are looking for more efficiently. Click on the post to open it, check that its content has not changed, **5** and click on the **Edit** link.

6. In the **Comments** module, click the **Add comment** link. **6**

7. The **Comment Editor** opens. Introduce a comment on your post to test it out **7** and click **Add comment**.

8. The comments made in your posts will be shown as follows: the author, e-mail address, and the site are shown on the left side and the date, time, and the content of the comment are shown on the right.

9. The **Author** module contains an expandable menu. If your blog has more than one author, a specific author can be selected from this menu. **8** Later on you will see how to invite new authors to the blog.

10. Go to the next exercise, where you will work with the **Revisions** module.

5

SEPTEMBER 8, 2013
Do you know the world could be better on a bike?

Everybody needs some time to think.

When everything around you is hectic and busy, there's nothing like a bike ride to give you some 'me time'... ...Whether you're on the way to work, riding for leisure or just trying to get a break from the kids, the world looks better from the saddle.

It's a cheap, easy and convenient way to get around and you'll be in good company, with thousands of people across Greater Bristol taking to their bikes.

THE LANGUAGE BARRIER IS TOO GREAT. HONK! HONK!

7

Comments

Add new Comment

| b | i | link | b-quote | del | ins | img | ul | ol | li | code | lookup | close tags |

proofread

We take your package in perfect condition, even if it rains!

Cancel   Add Comment

8

Comments

Add comment

Paul Adams   Submitted on 2013/01/17 at 10:45 am
mybike.wordp
ress.com   We take your package in perfect condition, even if it rains!
pauladams927@gmai
l.com
89.128.43.162

6

Comments

Add comment

No comments yet.

Comparing revisions and customizing the screen

WORDPRESS.COM MAKES BACKUP COPIES OF YOUR posts and files them so that you can access them at any moment. To do so you need only open the Revisions module and select the version you would like to restore.

1. For this exercise you should have the **Post editor** open for a post that has been updated on various occasions. Then, open the **Revisions** module and click on the oldest date (this is a link). 🔲

2. The revision window for the selected post opens, which shows the text with all the codes in the post. It also shows a list of revisions made. 🔲 Since the revision that we have selected is empty, we will click on the link of the next oldest post.

3. The content in the upper part of the screen is updated. The chosen post is selected in the column called **Old** in the **Revisions** section. The most recent post is selected in the column called **New**. 🔲 Click the **Compare revisions** button.

4. In the upper part of the window the HTML of both versions appear in different columns so that you can see the changes. 🔲 Change the selection in the **Old** column (in the lower part of the window) and click **Compare Revisions** again.

1

Revisions

16 January, 2013 @ 10:30 [Autosave] by Paul Adams
16 January, 2013 @ 9:43 by Paul Adams
16 January, 2013 @ 9:29 by Paul Adams

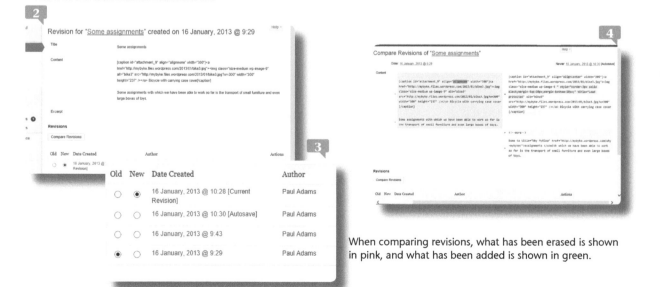

When comparing revisions, what has been erased is shown in pink, and what has been added is shown in green.

5. It is updated and, probably, the number of introduced changes will be reduced. The word **Autosave** might appear in brackets in some of the revisions as WordPress.com makes backup copies automatically. If you would like to go back to a previous version, you need only click the link on the left in the same row, **Restore**.

6. WordPress.com will send you back to the **Post editor** and will inform you in the header that this post has been restored. Click **Update** to complete the process.

7. Expand the **Screen Options** panel. In the **Number of Columns** section, select **1**.

8. Only the appearance of the **Editor** changes. The design of the page is not affected at all. Return to the two-column configuration, click on the upper right-hand corner of one of the modules and note how it contracts.

9. Now drag one of them to another part of the screen. You should see a broken line in the place where you would like to put it. Reorganize the post's screen at your will.

7

Number of Columns: ● 1 ○ 2

Editing Options
☐ Surprise me
☐ Show the feedback and progress sidebar after posting
☐ Use Zemanta to find related content (images, links, articles, & tags) to use in my posts. Your Zemanta API key is vzh3hsigsdhcrvergeszitaeu . Yo

Screen Options ⌃

Edit Post Add New

Post updated. View post

Some assignments

Permalink: http://mybyke.wordpress.com/2013/01/16/some-assignments/ Edit View Post Get Shortlink

Add Media 🔊 🖾   Visual Text

B I ⚊ ≡ ≣ ⟨⟨ ▤ ▥ ▦ ⌁ ▤ ♥ ⌕ ▦

5

Compare Revisions of "Some assignments"

These revisions are identical.

Older: 16 January, 2013 @ 9.29

Revisions

Compare Revisions

Old	New	Date Created	Author
	○	16 January, 2013 @ 10.28 [Current Revision]	Paul Adams
	○	16 January, 2013 @ 10.30 [Autosave]	Paul Adams
○	●	16 January, 2013 @ 9.43	Paul Adams
●	○	16 January, 2013 @ 9.29	Paul Adams

You can customize the layout of the posts screen. **8**

Publish

Categories

Format

Tags

Restore

6

16 January, 2013 @ 9.29   Paul Adams   Restore

Configuring and managing comments

BY DEFAULT, BLOGS IN WORDPRESS.COM ONLY allow comments from recognized users. This is to prevent spam, but can be changed easily from your Dashboard's Adjustments screen.

1. When a person tries to comment on a post in your blog they will find a form like this one. **1** To modify it, go to the **Dashboard** and click **Settings**.

2. Make any changes you would like in the **General Settings** screen **2** and click **Save Changes**.

3. Click on the secondary tab called **Discussion**. **3** The posts allow comments by default, but this can be changed in **Default Article Settings**. So users can make comments without identifying themselves, deactivate the option **Comment author must fill out name and e-mail**.

4. Note that the next option allows for restricting access to users of WordPress.com. **4** Make any further changes that you would like in this options screen. The **Prompt** field (in the last section) allows you to modify the text that will appear in the comments. **5** When you have finished, click **Save Changes**.

1

Leave a Reply

Email (required)   Address never made public

Name (required)

Website

☐ Notify me of follow-up comments via email.   Post Comment

2

General Settings

Site Title	mybike
Tagline	Test Site ✕

In a few words, explain what this site is about.

The short description is the one that appears below the blog's title. It should be concise and contain keywords.

The Settings options are distributed among various screens.

3

Settings

General

Writing

Reading

Discussion

Media

4

Other comment settings

☐ Comment author must fill out name and e-mail
☐ Users must be registered and logged in to comment
☐ Automatically close comments on articles older than 14 days
☑ Enable threaded (nested) comments 3 ☑ levels deep
☑ Break comments into pages with 50 top level comments per page and the last ☑ page di
by default

5. Obtain some comments on your blog and click the **Comments** tab on the **Dashboard**. 6

6. Comments awaiting approval are highlighted in yellow. 7 If the cursor is placed over one of them, its options are shown. Click the **Approve** option for one of the comments. 8

7. Now select the **Quick Edit** option for one of them.

8. You can edit a user's comment. Click **Cancel** and now select the **Edit** option for the same comment.

9. A screen opens that allows you to modify more data and also shows the **Comment History**. Click **View Comment**.

10. The post containing the comment appears in a new window. Close it and update the comment to return to the **Comments** screen.

11. Mark a comment as **Spam** and then click the link called **Pending** (in the header of the screen).

12. Click the selection box at the top of the table to select all comments. Expand the **Bulk Actions** menu and select **Approve**. 9

IMPORTANT

You can decide that after a certain amount of time users cannot comment on certain posts. You can define the level of nesting allowed, define the number of comments that will appear in the post by default (and in which order they appear), configure the notifications that will be sent to you by e-mail, decide that the comments of those users who have previously published comments need not pass through mediation. You can also create different criteria for the moderation of comments or for creating a comments blacklist (these will be marked as spam immediately).

Comments marked as Spam are saved in a file with the same name. They are not published.

Using the Zemanta module

IMPORTANT

In the **Additional Post Content** section in the **Personal Settings screen** (accessed from the tab called **Users**), the **Help me** section find related content (images, links, related articles, and tags) to use in posts. The **Powered by Zemanta!** option can be activated for use in all of your posts and pages.

ZEMANTA IS A SERVICE THAT IS available for free to WordPress.com users. It automatically searches for images and articles that are related to each post as it is written. It is an aid for enriching your posts.

1. Start a new post and open the **Screen Options** panel.

2. Activate the **Use Zemanta to find related content (images, links, articles, & tags) to use in my posts** option ⬛ and minimize the **Screen Options** panel.

3. Type a title and text for the post, but do not insert any images. Wait to see what **Zemanta** offers.

4. When you have finished, scroll down to the lower part of the screen to the new module called **Recommendations**. ⬛ Drag it to place it next to the **Post editor**.

5. All the images that appear in this module are completely free of copyright and can be published without a fee. They have been selected automatically using the words contained in the post that you are writing. Place the pointer over one of them to see a larger thumbnail, its source, and its details. ⬛

6. Click on an image that you think is appropriate for the post.

7. The image is inserted into the post and a window called **Image Settings** opens. Decide on a position for the image, correct the proposed caption (without erasing the credits), define the size, and click **Done**. **1**

8. At the bottom of the **Recommendations** panel are a series of articles that the service considers to be relevant to your post. **5** To improve the results, enter one or more keywords in the search field and press **Return**. **6** You will have better results if you use English names or words.

9. On placing the pointer over one of the links, an excerpt will appear. **7** If you click on it, a section called **Related articles** is inserted into the text. It contains the article's title, the source, and a link to the source. **8**

10. At the foot of the **Post editor** is a section called **Recommended Links** that should list various terms that appear in your text. Click the **Apply all** link. **9**

11. In the text a link is automatically created for each of the terms in the list. **10**

IMPORTANT

Each of the links that Zemanta proposes contains a small menu for other link options. Once expanded, you can click on the **Visit** link of any of them to open the recommended page and, thus, make a good selection.

W Cargo Bike ▼

W Freight bicycle

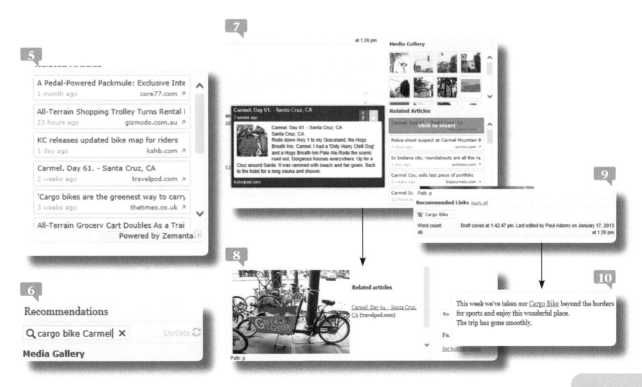

Creating a photo gallery on a page

A PHOTO GALLERY SHOWS A COLLECTION of thumbnails. When you click on one of them an enlarged view is shown on a carousel, allowing you to pass from one to another with just a click.

1. Go to the **Media Library** from its tab.

2. Click the **Add New** link and upload new photos to the **Upload New Media** box.

3. Select **Edit** for one of the images to show its options and make any necessary modifications. When finished, click **Update**.

4. Return to the Media Library through the corresponding tab and click the **Unattached** link.

5. Select all the photos by clicking on the selection box in the header, open the menu above it and select the **Attach to a post** option. Now click **Apply**.

6. In the **Find Posts or Pages** box, introduce a keyword to help you locate a page, click **Search**, select an option, and then click **Select**.

94

7. Open the page on which you attached the images and click **Add Media**. 9

8. A box opens called **Insert Media**, showing all the images that were attached from the library. Click on the tab called **Create Gallery**, select all the images, and then click on the **Create a new gallery** button. 10

9. Now you can drag and drop to reorder the images or you can reverse the default order. Select one of the images.

10. In the Gallery Settings section of the panel, you can change the characteristics of the gallery and customize each of the images. 11 Complete these fields as needed and click the **Insert Gallery** button.

11. Update the post and click the **Preview Changes** button to check the result. 12

12. Click on one of the images and check its appearance in the carousel. 13 Go through the images using the arrows on the sides. Click on one again to see it at full size.

13. To exit the gallery, click on the icon at the top left of the page and finish the exercise.

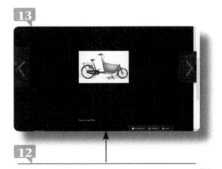

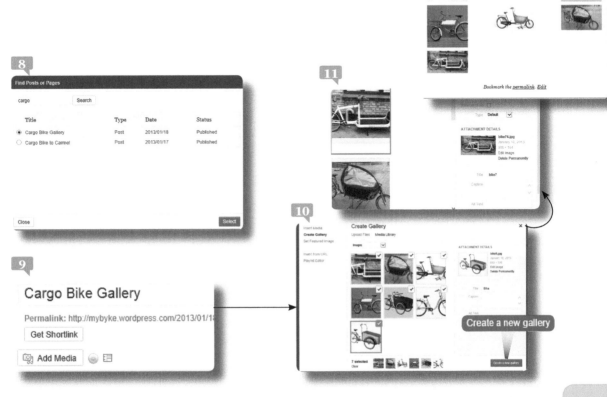

Editing a gallery and creating a slideshow

ONCE A PHOTO GALLERY HAS BEEN created, you can edit it, modify images, or convert it into a slideshow. In a slideshow, the images pass, fading from one to the next automatically.

1. You will continue working with the page containing the image gallery, so keep it open in the **Editor**. Click on the gallery and then click the **Edit Gallery** button in the top left-hand corner. [1]

2. You can access the gallery settings again. In the **Gallery Settings** section, keep the **Media File** option in the **Link To** field selected. [2]

3. Click the **Update Gallery** button, update the page, and preview the changes.

4. Click one of the thumbnails again to enlarge it in the carousel [3] and observe how, on clicking the image again, it passes on to the next one. [4]

5. Go back to the page's editing screen and enter the gallery settings box again.

Clicking on the second button that appears on selecting an inserted object will eliminate it.

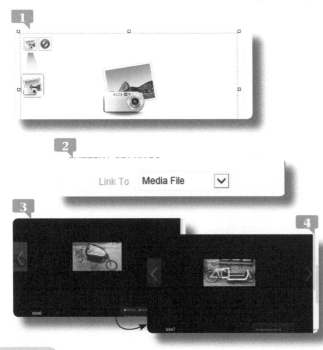

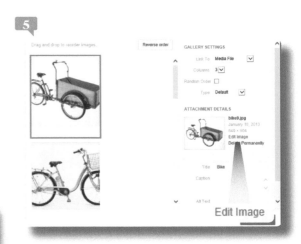

Once images have been attached, they can be edited at any time.

042

6. Click on any image to see how you can change the image's information. Do so if necessary.

7. Click the **Edit Image** link to the right of the thumbnail, in the **Attachment Details** section. 💬**5**

8. You can now edit the photograph. 💬**6** Click the **Scale Image** link, read the instructions, 💬**7** and introduce new dimensions if you wish, clicking **Scale** if you do so. Click on **Scale Image** to minimize it again. Now click the **Help** link in the **Image Crop** module.

9. Read the instructions and crop if necessary. 💬**8**

10. Note that the buttons in the image's header allow you to rotate and flip it as well as to undo or redo any action. When the image is ready, hide the image details and click the **Save** button.

11. Back to the Edit Gallery page, select the **Type** field and select the **Slideshow** option. 💬**9** Update the gallery by clicking in the corresponding button, update the page, and preview it.

12. A slideshow is shown on the same page automatically. 💬**10** If you click on it some controls appear that allow you to go forward, backward, or pause.

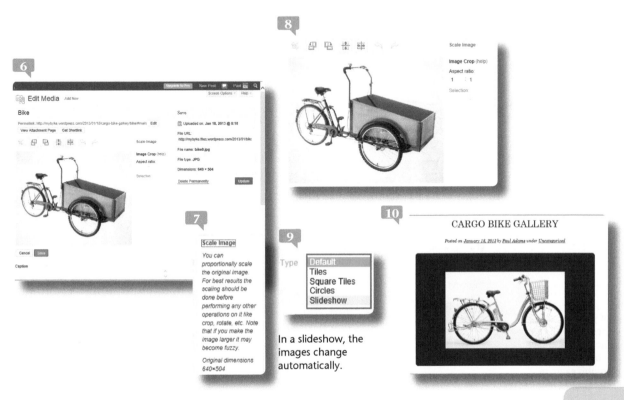

In a slideshow, the images change automatically.

Uploading photos and videos from Flickr

IF YOU HAVE A FLICKR ACCOUNT you can publish your photos and videos directly from it. In this exercise you will learn how to create an account and begin to share images from Flickr.

1. You will need a Flickr account, so if you do not yet have one, you can get one easily using your Google Account. Go to **www.flickr.com** and click the **Sign In** link.

2. Click the Google button in the **Sign in with** section, sign in with your username and allow information from Google to be used.

3. Fill in the next form and click **Continue**.

4. Click on link **1. Personalize your profile**, create a buddy icon following the instructions, if you wish, or keep the default one. Create a customized URL (adding easy to remember text) and customize your profile with the information you would like to give.

5. Click the **Upload your first photos** link.

Sign In

If you have a Yahoo! account you can access it and save yourself the first steps of this exercise.

You can also sign in to Flickr with your Facebook account.

Type a name in the **Choose your Flickr screen name** field and click **Check**.

6. Drag the photos to the window that appears or click the **Choose photos and videos to upload** button to browse for them.

7. Once they have been added, 🔴5 you can organize them by dragging them across the screen, 🔴6 click on their names to change them 🔴7 or change the description of the photo. 🔴8 If you select one of the images, you can use the panel on the left to add tags, 🔴9 identify people, add them to previously created albums, link to groups, or change the privacy settings.

8. Select all of the photos and click the **Add to sets** tab. Insert a name and a description for the new album in the dialog box that opens. Now click the **Create Set** button, select the album, and click the **Done** button.

9. When you have finished, click the **Upload Photos** button and confirm in the next box.

10. Hover your mouse over the icon for your account and click on the **Settings** option. 🔴10

11. Click the **Sharing and Extending** tab in the header and then on the **More Sites** tab.

12. Select the WordPress.com icon, fill in the form with your blog's details, and click the **Next** button. 🔴11

IMPORTANT

Tags in Flickr are separated by spaces and not with commas. Should you wish to create a tag consisting of two words, you should write its name between brackets.

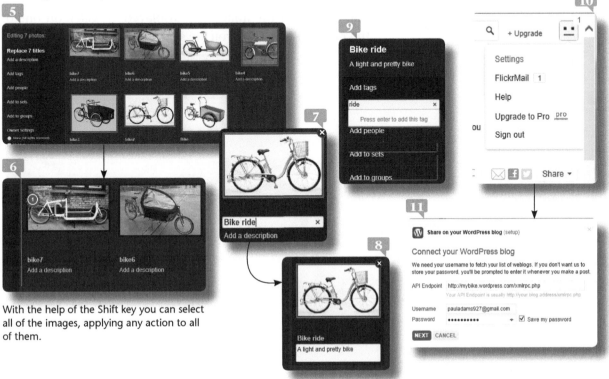

With the help of the Shift key you can select all of the images, applying any action to all of them.

Publishing Flickr photos and videos on your blog

ONCE YOU HAVE UPLOADED SOME PHOTOGRAPHS or a video to Flickr, you can publish them on your WordPress.com blog without having to access your site. You can also copy the URL and insert it into a new WordPress.com blog in the place you would like, which would give you greater control.

1. Go to your Flickr gallery, click the **Sets** link 🔲 and then click the thumbnail of the set created in the previous exercise. 🔲 Now click the **Share** button in the header. 🔲

2. Click the WordPress icon. 🔲

3. Insert a title and text for the post into the dialog box that opens. When you have finished click the **Post** button. 🔲

4. A new dialog box indicates that the set has been shared. Click the **Go to your WordPress blog** link.

5. You can now see the post on the title page of the blog. 🔲 Note if you need to change the text and click on the post.

6. Thumbnails of the images are displayed. 🔲 Click on one of the posts and see how you are sent to Flickr. 🔲

Your photostream

Photostream **Sets** Favorites Galler

Cargo bikes collection

When a Flickr photo set is published on a blog, no image appears on the title page.

7. Follow the same steps as in the previous exercise for uploading images and upload a video to Flickr.

8. In the gallery, click on the video to open it.

9. Instead of clicking on the **WordPress** button in the **Share** tab, select and copy its address from the browser's corresponding address box.

10. In another window, create a new blank post. Give it a title and type some text for the video, as well as any other information you like.

11. Paste the video link that you copied from Flickr in the place that you would like to insert the video.

12. Click the **Preview** button and observe how WordPress.com has inserted the video.

13. Go back to the post's screen and open the HTML editor.

14. Find the video's URL, copy the code's number and substitute the text for the following: [flickr video=VIDEO_NUMBER show_info=no]. Paste the video's number into the correct place to remove text automatically inserted by WordPress.com.

IMPORTANT

To get a customized code in Flickr, choose the **Grab the HTML/BBCode** option from the Share menu and click the **Personalize the video player** link, complete the form, and copy the code that is given.

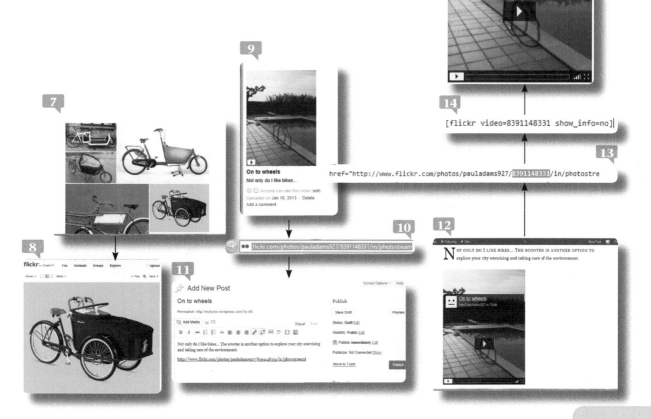

Publishing Vimeo and YouTube videos

IMPORTANT

The Share option can be used in both YouTube and Vimeo to obtain a customized embedding code. In YouTube you should use the Insert button and in Vimeo the Customized Embedding Options link. You need only select the desired options to obtain a code that embeds the video with specific dimensions or other characteristics.

THE AUTO EMBED FUNCTION (SELECTED BY DEFAULT) in the Media page under the Settings tab allows you to insert a video by copying its URL. Try it and learn how to customize the way the video is shown.

1. Find a video on YouTube that you would like to share.

2. Since YouTube does not offer a direct link for sharing on WordPress.com, you will do so another way. Click the **Share** button 1 and copy the link that appears. 2

3. Open a new post in another window of your WordPress.com blog, give it a title, type some text, and then paste the link.

4. Click the **Preview** button to check that the video plays perfectly 3 and watch it all.

5. It ends with related videos. Return to the Editor and change the URL for the following text: **[youtube= VIDEO URL &rel=0]**, substituting **VIDEO URL** for the right address. 4

6. Play the video and see how links to other related videos have been removed.

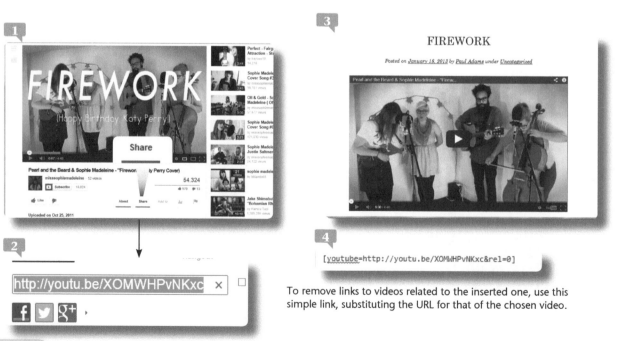

To remove links to videos related to the inserted one, use this simple link, substituting the URL for that of the chosen video.

7. Substitute the text at the end, **&rel=0]**, with **w=560&h=315]** and see how the size of the video has been modified.

8. You can give it any size by changing the values that correspond to width (**w**) and height (**h**). Publish the post.

9. Go to Vimeo in another window in your browser. Find a video that you would like to publish and copy its address from the browser's address bar, or select the **Copy video URL** option in its shortcut menu.

10. Paste the URL into a new post after giving it a title and inserting some text. Preview the result.

11. Go back to the video and select the **Copy embed code** option from the shortcut menu. Paste the copied code over the URL in the WordPress.com post.

12. Preview it to check how the size of the video box is modified. If you would like to use a customized size, you can use a short code. Copy the numeric values of the video's URL and substitute the code in the post with the following: **[vimeo NUMERIC_CODE w=350&h=200]**. However, change the text **NUMERIC_CODE** with the copied code.

13. You now know the code needed to customize the size of a video in Vimeo. End with publishing the post and check the result again.

IMPORTANT

You can also publish videos form Blip.tv, DailyMotion, Flickr, Google Video, and Hulu, as well as themes and lists from Spotify, by pasting the URL directly into a WordPress.com post or page. WordPress.com will make sure it's done correctly.

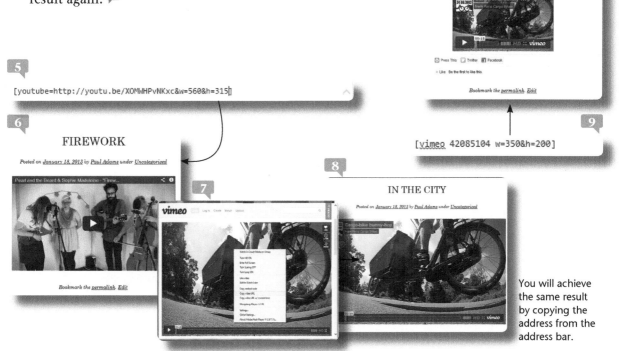

```
[youtube=http://youtu.be/XOMWHPvNKxc&w=560&h=315]
```

FIREWORK

Posted on *January 18, 2013* by *Paul Adams* under *Uncategorized*

Bookmark the *permalink*. *Edit*

IN THE CITY

Posted on *January 18, 2013* by *Paul Adams* under *Uncategorized*

```
[vimeo 42085104 w=350&h=200]
```

IN THE CITY

Posted on *January 18, 2013* by *Paul Adams* under *Uncategorized*

You will achieve the same result by copying the address from the address bar.

Creating a survey

THANKS TO THE INTEGRATED SERVICE CALLED Polldaddy, you can create surveys on your blog by filling in a simple form. You can ask questions that are open or closed, choose between various templates, and add images.

1. Click the **Feedbacks** tab on your WordPress.com Dashboard and select the **Polls** option. Keep the **Auto-create a new account** option selected and click the **Do it: I want some polls!** link.

2. The screen updates itself. Click the **Create a Poll Now** link.

3. You can already create your new poll. In the **New Poll** field, introduce the question you would like to ask.

4. Introduce three possible answers in the fields below.

5. You can add more possible answers if you wish. Click the **Add New Answer** button and introduce a new option.

6. Click the **Add an image** icon (the first on the right of the question).

7. Select the **Media Library** tab, click the **Show** link for the chosen image and click the **Insert into Post** link.

1

Links	hero guide
Pages	Have any technical quest
Comments	documentation pages are
Feedbacks	Feedbacks
Appearance	Polls
Users	Ratings
	Right Now

2

Polls in WordPress

To use polls in WordPress, you will need an account with our sister product, Polldaddy.com.

- ⦿ Auto-create a new account (recommended).
- ○ Import my existing PollDaddy account.

[Do it: I want some polls!]

3

Polldaddy Polls   Add New

Account imported.

Actions ▾   Apply   View All Polls ▾   Filter

☐ Poll

You haven't used our fancy plugin to create any polls for this blog!
Why don't you go ahead and get started on that?

[Create a Poll Now]

4

Answers

⇕ to work	▭ ▱ ♫ ×
⇕ to ride	▭ ▱ ♫ ×
⇕ to get away	▭ ▱ ♫ ×
⇕ to enjoy	× ▭ ▱ ♫ ×

[Add New Answer]

5   **6**

▭ ▱ ♫

▭

[Insert into Post]   Delete

You can insert an image, a video, or an audio file.

8. You can now see a thumbnail of the image to the left of the button. **7** Now repeat the process to insert an image for each of the answers.

9. The next button allows a musical theme to be added. The third button is for adding a video, and the last (an X) is for erasing the answer. Select the options you want in the **Results Display**, **Repeat Voting**, and **Comments** modules.

10. Using the arrowhead buttons, look at the different samples in the **Poll Style** panel. Select one. **8**

11. If you place the pointer over the sample, you will see how the results are displayed. **9** When you have finished, select the options you want in the **Save** panel, press the **Save poll** button. **10**

12. You will already be able to see the code of the created poll in the header. To its right, the **Embed Poll in New Post** button is activated. Click it. **11**

13. A post appears with the poll's code already embedded. **12** Give it a title, complete with the information you wish to give, add a featured image for the post, and publish it.

IMPORTANT

The Customized styles tab in the Polls screen allows you to design your own poll style. You can modify each of the components of the poll: the box, the question, the answers, the buttons, etc.

7

10
Save

☑ Randomize answer order
☑ Allow other answers
☐ Multiple choice
☑ Sharing

Save Poll

11
Poll created.

Why would you use a Cargo bike?

WordPress Shortcode: [polldaddy poll=6838755]   Embed Poll in New Post

Answers

to work
to ride
to get away
to enjoy

Add New Answer

Save
☑ Randomize
☑ Allow other
☐ Multiple ch
☑ Sharing

Results Disp
◉ Show result

8

9 of 20
Plastic Grey
Wide | Medium | Narrow

9

9 of 20
Plastic Grey
Wide | Medium | Narrow

12
Enter title here

Add Media

b i link b-quote del ins img ul ol li code more lookup
close tags proofread fullscreen

[polldaddy poll=6838755]

Publi
Save
Status
Visibili
Pu
Public
Move

You can also use the poll's code to insert it into a page, a comment, or a text widget.

Editing a poll

IMPORTANT

The second of the three **Add** buttons in Wordpress.com's Posts and Pages editors allow a previously created poll, as well as a new poll to be inserted.

ONCE YOU HAVE CREATED A POLL, you can edit it directly from Polldaddy's site or from WordPress.com through the Polls tab.

1. Let's see how the poll created in the previous exercise works. In the WordPress.com header in the **Dashboard**, click your blog's link.

2. The post will look more attractive if you had added a featured photo and an excerpt. Click on the poll to open it and check that the images you chose have indeed been embedded.

3. Select an option and click the **Vote** button.

4. The poll results are displayed as a bar graph. In our example a couple of users have voted. Click on the **Comments** link in the Poll module.

5. The poll opens on Polldaddy's site. Insert a comment and fill in the requested details.

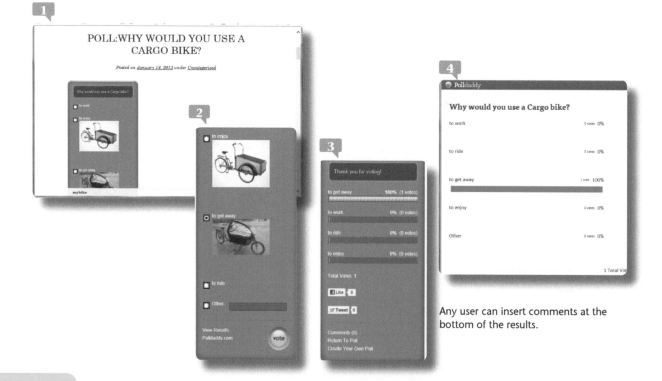

Any user can insert comments at the bottom of the results.

6. Click the **Sign In** button, sign in with your Wordpress.com account, open your e-mail and open the e-mail that should have been sent from Polldaddy. Copy the password and connect to the Polldaddy account. ▸6

7. Go to your Polldaddy **Dashboard**. From here you can set your profile for this site, create new polls, or edit already existing ones (among other options). ▸7 Place the pointer over the your poll's name and select the **Edit** option. ▸8

8. You can modify the attached media files. Click the **Media** button to the right of the question, ▸9 click the **Library** tab in the panel that opens, select another image, and click the **Insert** button.

9. Click the **Add New Answer** button and add another answer. ▸10

10. Click the **Save Settings** button and return to the **WordPress.com** Dashboard.

11. Click the **Feedbacks/Polls** tab and place the pointer over the name of the poll to reveal the options. Select the **Embed & Link** option. ▸11

12. The embedding codes will be shown for sharing the poll in other media. ▸12 Click the **Done** button, open the options again, and select the one called **Results** to see another view of the poll's graph.

IMPORTANT

You can configure the default settings for polls in the Polls Settings section in WordPress.com's Settings screen.

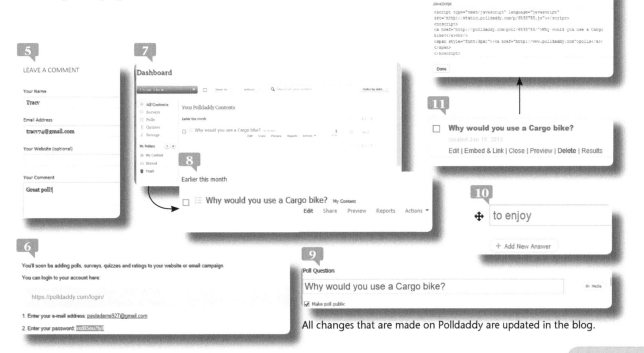

All changes that are made on Polldaddy are updated in the blog.

Inserting a contact form

YOU CAN INSERT A CONTACT FORM into any page or post on your blog. You can decide how many fields it should include and what type of answers it will allow in each.

1. If you have not already done so, it's now time to edit your **About** page. Open the **Pages** screen, place the pointer over the one in question to display its options, and then select **Edit**.

2. Once you have adjusted the content, click **Add a custom form** (the third icon from the left of the **Insert** block of icons). 1

3. The **Add a Custom Form** dialog box opens in a floating window 2 where you can configure the form that will be inserted. Pass the pointer over the **Name** field to display its options and click the **Edit** link. 3

4. Write the text you would like to appear in the **Label** field on the right. 4

5. Repeat the process to fill the other fields. 5

You can create forms that allow possible clients to request estimates, make inquiries, and to request customer support, for instance.

6. When you have filled in the fields, click the **Add a New Field** link to add another field to the questionnaire. **6**

7. Display its options, click the **Edit** link, and change the label to suit you.

8. Drop down the **Field type** menu and select **Checkbox**. **7**

9. A field is created with a check box. Create a new field, edit it, and go to the **Field Type** menu again.

10. Select the **Drop down** option **8** to add a drop-down menu.

11. Introduce an alternative in the **Option** field.

12. Click the **Add Another Option** link and add a new option in the field that is created.

13. Repeat the process to add all the necessary options, and if necessary, **9** add new fields to the form.

14. Display the options of a field you would like to move, click the **Move** link, and, when a floating label appears, drag it to the desired location. Click the **Add this form to my post** link.

15. Preview the page and check that the selection fields and options work correctly. **10** Publish the post.

IMPORTANT

The **Add E-mail Notification** tab in the **Add a Custom Form** dialog box allows you to determine if contact necessary notifications should be sent to an e-mail address that is not that of the author, as well as changing the message title of the notification sent.

You can modify the text of your user form directly in its code, which is inserted into the post.

6

Comment (required)

Add a new field

8

Edit this new

Label

Field type

| Checkbox |
| Drop down |
| Email |
| Name |
| Radio |
| Text |
| Textarea |
| Website |

Save this field

7

Edit this new

Label

Field type

| Checkbox |
| Drop down |
| Email |
| Name |
| Radio |
| Text |
| Textarea |
| Website |

Save this field

9

Edit this new field

Label   Approximate weight

Field type   Drop down

Option   From 0 to 5 kilos

                 From 5 to 15 kilos

                 From 15 to 30 kilos   ×

Add another option

☐ Required?

10

Paul Adams

Email (required)

pauladams927@gmail.com

Website

http://mybike.wordpress.com

☐ **Collection address**

Approximate weight

From 0 to 5 kilos
From 5 to 15 kilos
From 15 to 30 kilos

Editing a contact form

SHOULD YOU WISH TO MODIFY A contact form that is already inserted into your page or post, you should do so from its code. In this exercise we will learn how to change the label or the field types, among other things.

1. To edit the form created in the previous exercise, open the post in the Page editor.

2. Were you to access the form's editor by clicking on the **Insert custom form** button you would find yourself in a new template 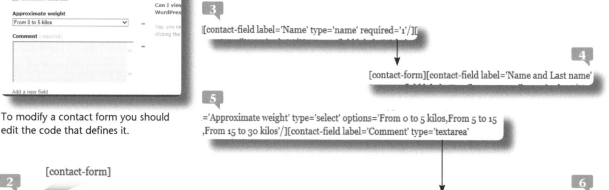 and would need to create the form again, incorporating the changes. To avoid this you can introduce corrections into the code itself. Let us first analyze it. The code starts with a label that identifies it as a contact form: [**contact-form**] and ends with its closing version: [**/contact-form**]. You cannot modify the content of either.

3. Each field follows this basic structure: [**contact-field label='Name' type='name' required='1'/**] where only the information between normal brackets can be modified. The text **contact-field label** assigns the label to the field and **type** indicates what type of field it is. The value **1** referring to the text **required** designates that an answer is compulsory. Should you wish to indicate that an answer is optional, you should erase the whole code.

1

Form builder   Email notifications

Here's what your form will look like

How does

Name (required)

By adding
to submit f
automatica
feedback w

Email (required)

Can I add

Website

Sure thing.
textarea, r

☐ Collection address

Can I viev
WordPres

Approximate weight

From 0 to 5 kilos

Yep, you ca
clicking the

Comment (required)

Add a new field

To modify a contact form you should edit the code that defines it.

3

[contact-field label='Name' type='name' required='1'/][

4

[contact-form][contact-field label='Name and Last name'

5

='Approximate weight' type='select' options='From 0 to 5 kilos,From 5 to 15 ,From 15 to 30 kilos'/][contact-field label='Comment' type='textarea'

2

[contact-form]

[contact-form][contact-field label='Name' type='name' required='1'/][contact-field label='Email' type='email' required='1'/][contact-field label='Website' type='url'/] [contact-field label='Collection address' type='checkbox'/][contact-field label='Approximate weight' type='select' options='From 0 to 5 kilos,From 5 to 15 kilos,From 15 to 30 kilos'/][contact-field label='Comment' type='textarea' required='1'/[/contact-form] This i

displayed on your blog's front page in the order they're published, pages are better suited for more timeless content that you want to be easily accessible, like your About

📅 Published on: Jan 15, 201

Move to Trash

][/contact-form]

Parent

6

='Approximate weight' type='select' options='From 0 to 5 kilos,From 5 to 15 ,From 15 to 40 kilos'/][contact-field label='Comment' type='textarea'

Now, with this information, select the text of a label field and modify it. 🔲

4. The different codes for file types are as follows:

- **name**: Creates a name field.

- **text**: Creates a single-line text field.

- **textarea**: Creates a multi-line field.

- **e-mail**: Creates a field that only accepts an e-mail address.

- **url**: Creates a field that only accepts a URL address.

- **select**: Creates a drop-down option field.

- **Checkbox**: Creates a check box field.

- **Radio**: Creates a multiple options field with corresponding selection buttons.

5. Fields that permit various options are found after the **options** label as follows: [contact-field label='FIELD LABEL' type='select' options='OPTION1,OPTION2'/]. 🔲 Note that the options labels are separated by commas without spaces between them. Edit the names you need to change for your form or add a new option. 🔲

6. To add a field with buttons, introduce this code: [contact-field label='FIELD LABEL' type='radio' options='OPTION1,OPTION2'/], but substitute the text in capitals for the concepts they should describe. 🔲 You can insert this between the two fields where you want it to be positioned, but it should always come before the closing label: [/contact-form]. When you have finished, update the page and open it. 🔲

7. When a reader completes a form, you will receive an e-mail and will be able to access the information using the **Feedbacks** tab in your blog's Dashboard. 🔲

7

required='1'/][contact-field label='Pick up at our store?'type='radio'options='Yes,No'/][/contact-form] This is an example of a page.

9

	Dashboard	Feedbacks		Screen Options ▾	H...
	Store	Messages (1)			
	Posts	Bulk Actions ▾ Apply Show all dates ▾ Filter		Search Feed	
	Media				
	Links	☐ From	Message	Date	
	Pages	☐ Tracy McDonalds soscost@gmail.com	[mybike] About I am interested in getting a quote for a monthly shipment in San Francisco	2013-01-21 @ 9 1 AM	
	Comments	http://mybike.wordpress.com			
	Feedbacks	89.128.43.162	Collection address		
	Feedbacks	http://mybike.wordpress.com/about/	Approximate weight From 5 to 15 kilos		
	Polls		Pick up at our store? Yes		
	Ratings				

8

http://mybike.wordpress.com

☐ **Collection address**

Approximate weight

From 0 to 5 kilos ▾

Comment (required)

Pick up at our store?

☐ Yes

☐ No

Submit »

For editing other aspects of a contact form you will need to download a CSS customization update.

Activating and configuring ratings

WORDPRESS.COM ALLOWS YOU TO ACTIVATE A rating system for posts, comments, and pages. You can also modify its appearance and customize labels among other things.

1. Click the **Ratings** option in the **Feedbacks** tab, **1** and then click **Settings**.

2. Select the **Show Ratings on / Posts** check box, **2** open the menu and select the **Below each blog post** option. **3**

3. Activate the **Front Page, Archive pages,** and **Search Results** option. Keep the **Above each blog post** option selected and save the changes.

4. Click the **Comments** tab, **4** activate the ratings in the **Comments** option **5** and save the changes.

5. Go to your blog and observe how the ratings are displayed above each post. **6**

6. When you place the pointer over a star, the corresponding ratings are shown. **7** The greater the number of stars, the higher the ratings. Vote on all posts.

The **Ratings** options allow you to set up a scoring system for posts, pages, and comments.

In all cases you can place the ratings above or below the object in question.

7. On voting, you are shown the total number of votes cast. **8** Now open one of the posts.

8. As expected, the rating is shown above the post. **9**

9. Return to the **Ratings** screen and go to the settings window; click the **Posts** tab and click **Advanced Settings**. **10**

10. Select the **Nero Rating** option and check its appearance in the **Preview**. **11** Go back to the **5 Star Rating** presentation.

11. You can change the color, size, and image in the **Rating Style** module. In the **Text Layout and Font** module, you can change the ratings' text. The **Customize Labels** module allows you to change each of the labels. **12** You will not be able to see many of the labels until you have installed the **Ratings** widget.

12. Save the changes and click the **Ratings** option in the **Feedbacks** tab.

13. Return to the title page of the blog and check that the labels have been changed.

IMPORTANT

The **i** icon to the right of the rating opens a box that displays the favorite posts and allows you to filter the favorites by the day, week, or month.

★★★☆☆ **i** 1 Vote

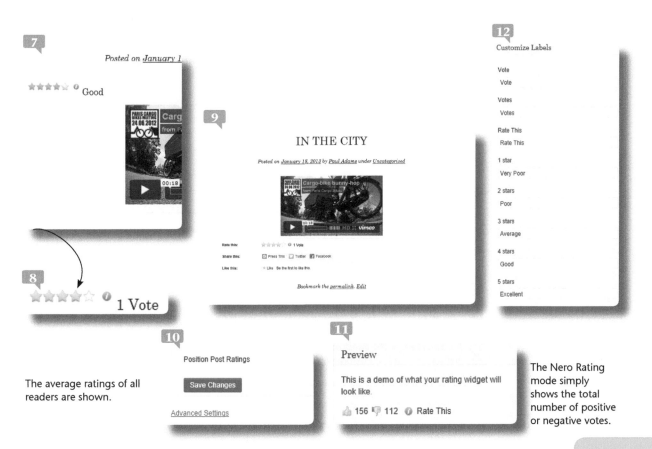

The average ratings of all readers are shown.

The Nero Rating mode simply shows the total number of positive or negative votes.

Choosing the appropriate theme for your blog

THE APPEARANCE SCREEN ON YOUR BLOG'S Dashboard allows you to preview the different themes, browse through them with various filters, preview their effect on your blog, and, finally, to apply whichever you choose.

1. Click the **Appearance** tab on your blog's Dashboard and note the many themes available. **1**

2. Click the **Live Preview** link **2** of any of them to see the effect it would have on your blog. **3** Click the **Cancel** button to return to the previous page.

3. The links in the **Available Themes** section allow you to browse through the themes at random, in alphabetical order, the most popular, the newest, the *Premium* (these have a price), those that have been recently selected, and, finally, some created by collaborators and partners of WordPress.com. **4** Try it.

4. If you click the **Details** link for one of the samples, you will see a short description. **5**

204 *items*

Trending | A-Z | Popular | Newest | Premium | Friends of WP.com

Browse themes trending right now based on activations, popularity, and site traffic.

204 items

Minimalizine
Activate   Live Preview   Details

Misty Lake
Activate   Live Preview   Details

mybike
Test Site

Latest News

You can set up various search filters.

January 15, 2013 | 0 ...
Poll:Why v   Available Themes

☆☆☆☆☆ 0 F   Trending | A-Z | Popular | Newest | Premium | Friends of WP.com

January 15, 2013 | 0 ...   *Browse themes trending right now based on activations, popularity, and site traffic.*
In the city

☆☆☆☆☆ 0 1 Vote

January 15, 2013 | 0 Comments
Firework

☆☆☆☆☆ 0 1 Vote

Koi

Activate   Live Preview   Details

January 15, 2013 | 0 Comments
On to wheels

This light and colorful theme provides a beautiful backdrop for your WordPress site with delicate, hand-drawn illustrations. Enjoy

Delicious Magazine

Live Preview
Delicious magazi...
Purchase ($75.00)   Live Preview   Details

You can preview the effect of all themes on your blog before you apply it.

114

5. Click **Activate** and a description of the selected theme appears in the header. ⬛ The **Read more about** link offers more specific information. Click it and then in the **Features** section on the new page, click on the **Custom Header** link. ⬛

6. In this way, all themes that permit the customization of the header are displayed. Choose one for your blog.

7. A presentation of the chosen theme is displayed. Hover your mouse over the image of this theme and click **Live Demo**. ⬛

8. Click the blog's different tabs and links to see how the theme looks ⬛ and then close the page to return to the showcase. Continue browsing until you make a final choice. Then click the **Use This Theme** button and **Activate** button to apply the selected theme.

9. You are sent back to the **Manage Themes** screen of your blog where you will see that the theme is already selected. ⬛ Click the **Visit Site** link in the header to access your blog and view the changes made.

10. Note the most important problems that your blog has with this theme. In your case, you have chosen a theme that needs a featured image for each post. ⬛ For posts that use a video instead of an image, you will take a video still frame, crop it, and use it as a featured image. Make the necessary adjustments to the posts before moving on to customizing the theme.

Customizing a theme

THE PREVIEW SCREEN'S CUSTOMIZE button in the Manage Themes screen allows you to configure the title page, the header, the colors and the background of the blog, among other things.

1. Go back to the **Appearance** screen on the blog's Dashboard and click on the **Customize** button in the preview of the current theme.

2. Your blog appears  with a customization panel on the right-hand side. Click the **Site Title & Tagline** tab.

3. You can change the blog's title and summary or hide them both (by deactivating the **Display Header Text** option). Click the **Colors** tab and click the Select Color button in the **Header Text Color** option.  Then make a selection for the background color  and check the result.

4. The **Background Image** section also allows you to upload an image from your computer. Click the **No Image** field and then click the **Select File** button.

5. Choose the image file you want in the **Select file(s) to upload by mybike.wordpress.com** and click **Open**.

You can use an image that contains the blog's title and hide the headline text by deactivating the **Display Header Text** in the **Site Title & Tagline** section.

6. If you have the **No Repeat** option selected in the **Background Repeat** section, it is likely that some part of the original background will remain uncovered. To avoid this, select one of the tile options. [8]

7. If you change the **Background Position**, a different segment of the chosen image will be shown. Try it and make a selection.

8. Click the **Static Front Page** tab and select the **A static page** option from the **Front page displays** section.

9. Expand the **Front Page** menu and select a page to be used as the blog's title page. [10] Wait to see the result in the preview. [11]

10. Expand the **Posts Page** menu and select the **About** page or another one, if you prefer. [12]

11. You cannot see the result in the preview. Click the **About** tab and note how all the posts are now visible. The correct thing to do would be to change the name of this page to something like **Blog.** For the next exercises, return to the latest posts option, although you can change them later if you wish. Click **Save and publish** to save the change, and then click **Close.**

If you set a tile background, make sure that the background is properly covered.

You can set any page as your site's front page, maintaining the recent posts (the blog) as an additional page.

Adding widgets

SHOULD YOU WISH TO WORK WITH you blog's widgets, you should expand the menu in the Appearance tab and select the appropriate option. You can insert new widgets, edit or erase existing ones. You can also remove one without losing its customizations.

1. Go to the **Appearance** screen and click the **Widgets** tab.

2. The largest part of the screen is occupied with the **Available Widgets** module. These are all the widgets that can be added to your blog.

3. The **Primary Sidebar** module contains the widgets that have been applied to your blog and shows other possible locations for your widgets, depending on the theme being used. There is a module at the bottom that is empty be default called **Inactive Widgets** where you can save widgets for later use.

4. Click the arrowhead button called **Categories** in the **Primary Sidebar** module.

5. You can change the title that will appear on the blog and customize other options. Make any changes and click **Save**.

1

Appearance

Themes
Widgets
Menus
Theme Options
Header
Background
Custom Design
Mobile

6. Click the panel called **Meta** and drag it to the **Inactive Widgets** module.

7. Expand the **Secondary Sidebar** module, select the **Author Grid** widget and drag it there.

8. Give it a name, select **Display all authors (including those who have not written any posts)** option and save the changes.

9. Add the **Blogs I Follow** and the **RSS Links** widgets as well.

10. The **Text** widget allows any text or HTML code to be introduced, while the **Image** widget allows an image to be inserted by indicating its URL. An image can also be linked to another address. These are two easy ways of introducing additional content into your site. For instance, you could insert the embedded code of a previously created poll or that of a video. You will do the latter.

11. Make any necessary adjustments and then open your blog and check the location, appearance, and performance of the bars containing the widgets.

053

IMPORTANT

The **Gravatar Profile** widget allows you to include a reduced version of your Gravatar Profile on your site.

Gravatar Profile

Display a mini version of your Gravatar Profile

In the theme that you have used, the secondary bar is placed in a third column on the right.

Creating a menu

THE MENUS SCREEN ALLOWS YOU TO create menus with the exact content desired. You can create menus of pages, categories or tags, or links to other sites. You can order them as you wish and choose their location.

1. Open the **Menus** screen from the **Appearance** tab on your blog's Dashboard. 🗨1

2. Type a name in the **Menu Name** field 🗨2 and then click the **Create Menu** button. 🗨3

3. In the **Pages** module, select the pages that you would like to include in your menu by clicking their check boxes. Then click **Add to Menu.** 🗨4

4. As a test, insert the URL of any site into the **Custom Links** module, give it a name and click **Add to Menu.** 🗨5

5. Make a selection from the **Categories** module and click **Add to Menu.** 🗨6

6. You can reorganize the elements of the menu simply by dragging them. If you place an element to the right of another, it

🗨1

📋 Feedbacks	
🗔 Appearance	Themes
👥 Users	Widgets
🛠 Tools	**Menus**
⚙ Settings	Theme Options
◂ Collapse menu	Header
	Background
	Custom Design
	Mobile

🗨2

+

Menu Name | Custom Menu | ✕

Create Menu

🗨3

Create Menu

The menu's name does not appear in the blog and is only used for managing content.

🗨4

Pages

Most Recent   View All   Search

☑ Why MyBike
☑ About
  ☑ Advertising
☐

Select All   Add to Menu

🗨5

Custom Links

URL   /nourishesall.blogspot.com.es

Label   Nourishes All   ✕

Add to Menu

Custom links allow another site to be included in your menu.

🗨6

Categories

Most Used   View All   Search

☐ Uncategorized
☑ Best commissions

Select All   Add to Menu

will be placed on a lower level.  Click the arrowhead of one of the elements in the menu to expand it. Then insert label text and expand the **Screen Options** module in the header.

7. You can also include tabs and labels in your menu, as well as other advanced options. Select the **Labels** and **Description** options and introduce a description in the field that appears.

8. Click **Save Menu**.

9. You must now decide where to place the menu. In the **Theme Locations** module, expand the **Primary Menu** field, select the menu that you created, and click **Save**.

10. Go to your blog, note the change in the menu, place the pointer over one of the menus with secondary elements, and see how they look.

11. On clicking the customized link, you are sent to its website.

12. Go back to the **Menu** screen and click on the + tab. Create a new customized menu and add labels or any other content from the modules on the left. Save the changes.

13. In the **Theme Locations** panel, select one as a main menu and the other as the secondary menu. Check the result. Finally, reorganize the menus as you prefer.

054

The content of the **Title Attributes** field appears as a floating label when the pointer is placed over the element containing it in the menu.

Other ways of modifying appearance

THE OPTIONS IN THE APPEARANCE SECTION also allow you to change the fonts used for your blog's title, the default text size, the color of the links, the header, and the background. You can also access the advanced options (for a fee) in Custom Design.

1. Click the **Themes Options** secondary tab in the **Appearance** section on the Dashboard. 🔲

2. You can choose a font to replace the current one. Expand the **Title Font Family** menu and make a selection. 🔲 Unfortunately it does not show a sample of the appearance, although you can go back to the original font.

3. Expand the next **Base Font Size** menu, and select a base text size. 🔲

4. Now click on the **Select a Color** button and select a shade that suits your blog. 🔲

5. When you have finished, click the **Save Changes** button and check the result. 🔲

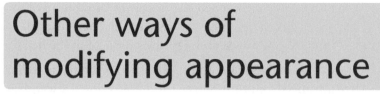

1

- ▣ Feedbacks
- ▣ Appearance   Themes
- ▣ Users   Widgets
- ▣ Tools   Menus
-                       **Theme Options**
- ▣ Settings   Header
- ◂ Collapse menu   Background
-                       Custom Design
-                       Mobile

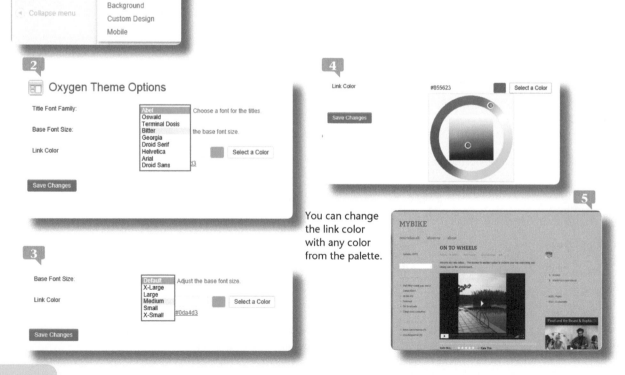

2

▣ Oxygen Theme Options

Title Font Family: Abel / Oswald / Terminal Dosis / Bitter / Georgia / Droid Serif / Helvetica / Arial / Droid Sans   Choose a font for the titles

Base Font Size: the base font size.

Link Color   Select a Color

Save Changes

3

Base Font Size: Default / X-Large / Large / Medium / Small / X-Small   Adjust the base font size.

Link Color   #0da4d3   Select a Color

Save Changes

4

Link Color   #855623   Select a Color

Save Changes

You can change the link color with any color from the palette.

5

MYBIKE

ON TO WHEELS

6. When you have finished, click the secondary tab, **Header**, which is also in the **Appearance** section.

7. Select another image. Click **Browse** to select one from your computer or **Choose Image** to select one from your Media Library. You should click the **Upload** button and then you can crop it after, although it is best to load images that have already been cropped to the correct size. 🔲 To finish the process, click the **Crop and Publish** button.

8. You can see how the new header looks and, if your theme allows for it, the Random option is activated. This allows each page to show a different image at ramdom. If your theme allows, activate it 🔲 and save the changes.

9. Next, click the **Background** tab, which is also in the **Appearance** section. You will see that it also has the customization options that you are familiar with.

10. Click the **Custom Design** secondary tab.

11. The update with the same name appears. Its price is shown in the header. Click the **Fonts** tab and change the fonts using the available menus, 🔲 just to see how it works. 🔲 You would need to buy an update to apply the changes.

12. The CSS tab allows you to create a style sheet in CSS code, although it also requires the update. Go back to your blog and check that it still has the original appearance.

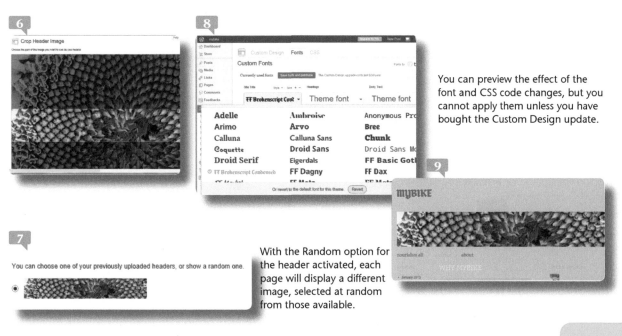

You can preview the effect of the font and CSS code changes, but you cannot apply them unless you have bought the Custom Design update.

With the Random option for the header activated, each page will display a different image, selected at random from those available.

Setting the appearance on mobiles

WORDPRESS.COM ASSIGNS A THEME FOR MOBILES by default. Not all themes adapt well to these devices, so if your blog's theme is incompatible, it will be substituted for Minileven, which is based on Twenty Eleven. However, you can disable the theme for mobiles, change the font used, and decide to display the complete posts or only their excerpts.

1. You will need a mobile phone with Internet access for this exercise. If you do not have one, read the following two exercises before working with this one and simulate it by changing your browser's user agent for that of iPhone. Click the **Appearance** tab and then the **Mobile** secondary tab. 🔲

2. You will probably have the **Enable mobile theme** option activated by default. 🔲 This will allow the original theme to be displayed on a modern mobile provided that you are using a theme that is adapted for mobiles such as the one you are using in this example. You will find the appropriate themes on the following page: **http://theme.wordpress.com/themes/features/responsive-width/**. If your theme does not have the **Responsive with** feature, the **Minileven** theme will be shown

The second theme option for mobiles allows you to choose between showing excerpts of the posts only or showing the full content.

by default. **Minileven** is an adaptation of **Twenty Eleven**. It maintains the customized header.

3. Go to your blog from your mobile and check the result. 3

4. Take into account the fact that if the mobile is an old one it will display a very basic theme that prioritizes loading times and information on the blog's content. In the **Enable mobile theme** field in the Dashboard's **Mobile** screen, select the **No** option. 4 Click **Update** and also update your blog on your mobile telephone.

5. The theme adapted to mobile devices is no longer displayed and, in our case, we have lost the background image. 5 This option causes slower loading, and old devices will not be able to read or upload your blog.

6. Reactivate the theme for mobiles and click the **Yes** option in the **Enable excerpts on front page and on archive pages** field to show excerpts of the posts instead of the full posts. Update it in WordPress.com. On your mobile, update the blog's screen and check the changes. 6

7. Go to the bottom of the blog on your mobile and click the **View Full Site** link. 7

8. The same version is shown as when the theme is deactivated. Now click the **View Mobile Site** link to go back to the mobile version.

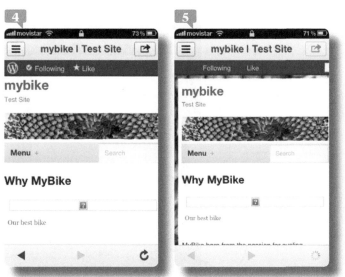

When the **Enable excerpts on front page and on archive pages** is deactivated the full version of the posts are shown on the front page of the blog's mobile version.

The user can go to the full version at any time using the **View Full Site** link.

Download and use Wordpress.com for iPad

WORDPRESS.COM HAS A SPECIAL APPLICATION FOR both iPad and iPhone. This complete program can be downloaded from the App Store and should be configured with the details of your account once installed on the device.

1. Go to the App Store from your iPad and search Wordpress.com. Once you find the application, you need to download and install it by clicking on the **Free** and **Install App** links.

2. Once finished the installation, click on **Open** to access to Wordpress.com.

3. In the first screen, you can choose one option if you already have a blog or if you want to start a new one. As we already have our blog, click on the **Add Wordpress.com Blog** button, type your username and your password and click on **Sign In**.

4. Allow the notifications on your device by clicking on **OK** and, in the **Select Blogs** screen, choose your blog and click on the **Add Selected** button.

5. Now you can see the posts screen. In the left panel, click on the **View Site** option to go to the blog and see the appearance for the iPad.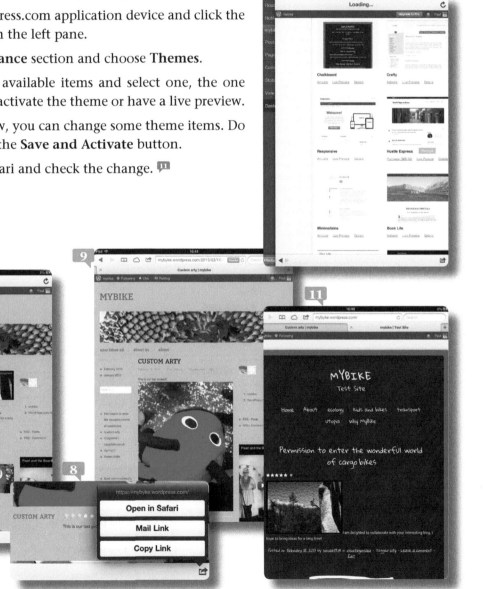

6. The panel on the left of the screen shows the main commands for log management, as in the online version of WordPress.com. You can check if the blog is well displayed in a browser using the icon at the bottom right of the screen. Click on it and click **Open in Safari**.

7. The result is excellent and immediate. Click on any of the links in the blog to make sure they work properly.

8. Return to the Wordpress.com application device and click the **Dashboard** option in the left pane.

9. Click on the **Appearance** section and choose **Themes**.

10. Browse through the available items and select one, the one you like. You can activate the theme or have a live preview.

11. From the live preview, you can change some theme items. Do it and then click on the **Save and Activate** button.

12. Open the blog in Safari and check the change.

Previewing appearance on mobile devices

FIREFOX ALSO OFFERS THE POSSIBLITY TO download an add-on called User Agent Switcher from its website. It allows you to simulate browsing with other browsers and devices, provided that you supply your user agent code.

1. Safari allows you to preview the appearance of your blog on iPad. You will have noticed that the Development menu offers the possibility to see any website as it appears on many other devices. As Safari is an Apple application, it gives priority to Apple devices. Go to the **addons.mozilla.org** website.

2. Use the search bar on the website to find the **User Agent Switcher** add-on.

3. When the panel appears, click the **Add to Firefox** button.

4. Confirm that you would like to install this software.

5. Complete the installation by restarting you computer when the application asks you to.

Once the add-on has been downloaded, you should restart the application to be able to use it.

If you would prefer not to make a shortcut on the browser's menu bar, you can access the add-on from the Tools menu.

6. When you return to Firefox, right-click on the toolbar and select the **Customize** option. **3**

7. Find the **User Agent Switcher** icon and drag it to the bar. **4**

8. Close the dialog box and click on the button that you added to your browser.

9. Just a few examples are displayed by default: some versions of Internet Explorer, search robots, and iPhone. **5** Select this option and open your blog. **6**

10. If you would like to check the effect in any other browser or device, you should locate its user agent. You can do so with a Google search or by going directly to a service like **useragentstring.com** or **myuseragentstring.com**, for example. Once you have found the user agent code, copy it **7** and expand the **User Agent Switcher** menu again.

11. Select the **Edit User Agents** option.

12. In the dialog box called **General**, click the button called **New** and select the **New User Agent** option.

13. Insert the user agent details you have **8** and click the **OK** button in this box and in the previous one.

14. Expand the **User Agent Switcher**, select the agent that was created, and reload the page to check the result. **9**

IMPORTANT

The user agent is an application that, on connecting to a website, identifies the client by sending a string of text to the server. This string gives information about the browser or application, its version, the device, and the language. When a string of text identifying the user agent from other devices is given to a browser, you can obtain an approximate version of the appearance of a website on other devices and applications.

The add-on includes a few agents as examples. You should find any others that you wish to use.

Publishing WordPress for iOS from the mobile

WORDPRESS.COM OFFERS APPLICATIONS FOR MOBILES THAT allow you to publish all sorts of content from wherever you happen to be. Download the right one for your mobile device.

1. If you would like to publish new content from anywhere and have a smartphone or a tablet, you must download the right application for your device. Go to the **Mobile** screen in the **Appearance** tab 1 and click on one of the thumbnails of devices at the bottom of the **Mobile Apps** section. 2

2. A page opens with information about the mobile applications that will allow you to publish on WordPress.com. As you will see, there are applications designed for iOS, Android, BlackBerry, Windows Phone, Nokia, and WebOS. 3 If you click on any of the links you will be sent directly to an information page on the application 4 from where you will be able to access the download page. 5

3. We have downloaded **WordPress for iOS (by Automattic)**. To start working you must click the **Add WordPress.com Blog** option. 6

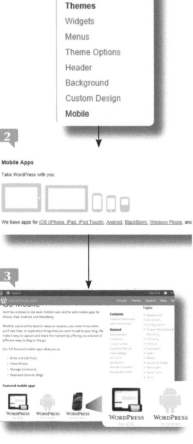

Although you can access the application's download page directly from your WordPress.com Dashboard, it is much simpler to do so directly from your device.

130

4. Provide the details requested in the log-in screen 🖪 and click **Enter** to start a WordPress.com session.

5. Once the session has started, you should select the blog you would like to work with from the device, which, in your case, is the only one associated with your user. Click the **Add Selected** button.

6. The application loads the blog's content, and the posts are immediately shown on the screen. 🖪 If you click on the title of a post or page, you will be able to edit it. 🖪

7. Although the text is displayed in HTML mode, it is very easy to use. When you click on the text, the **Text Editor** toolbar appears. We will talk about how to use it in the following exercise.

8. In the menu that is accessed from the icon in the top left-hand corner of the screen, 🖪 you have the same features as on the WordPress.com website. You can search for and edit posts, pages, and comments, check statistics, see the blog (**View Site**) or even access your blog's Dashboard 🖪 on WordPress.com with all of its features. These features can be accessed from a convenient icon menu. If you have the application, click this option and try it out for yourself. 🖪

> ## IMPORTANT
>
> The welcome page of WordPress for iOS 3.1, allows you to add a WordPress.com blog, as well as a WordPress.com blog with its own domain. You can also create a completely new blog.

Creating a post from an iPhone

IN THIS EXERCISE YOU WILL CREATE A POST from an iPhone and will become familiar with the basic functioning of the text editor for the iPhone.

1. In the WordPress for iOS **Posts** screen, click the **New Post** button in the top right-hand corner.

2. Insert a title and then type the tags in the following field.

3. Click the **Categories** field and note how, in this case, you can choose between those that already exist or can create a new one by clicking on the **Plus (+)** button. Select an option and click the **New Post** button.

4. Click the post's body text field to access the editor and rotate the device so that you can write more comfortably. You will see that the **Text** method is used.

5. Type your text. To write in italics you must click on the tool with the letter **I**.

6. The labels <em></em> are inserted and you should type the text to be displayed in italics between them. As the cursor is already in the correct place, simply type the text.

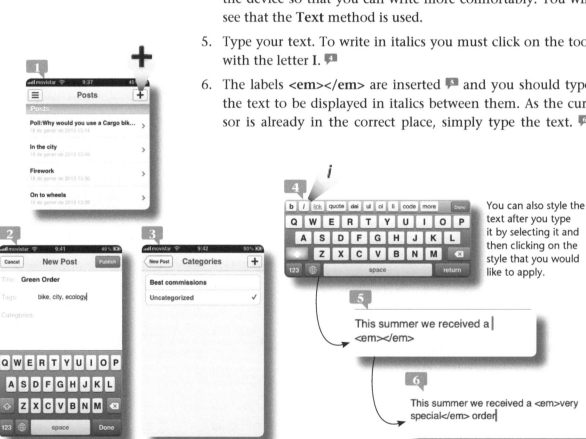

You can also style the text after you type it by selecting it and then clicking on the style that you would like to apply.

This summer we received a
<em></em>

This summer we received a <em>very special</em> order

Then place the cursor behind the closing label and continue to type.

7. You will now introduce a link. When you reach the appropriate place click the **Link** button.

8. In the **Make a Link** box, type the text that will display the link in the first text field. In the second field type the URL, and then click **Insert**.

9. To check that the result is correct, click the **Done** button to hide the keyboard and then the **Preview** button (the eye icon, which is the third button at the bottom of the screen). Then click the **Edit** button (the pencil icon) to continue. Insert a line break where you would like to insert an image, press the **Done** button to close the keyboard, and click the **Insert Image** button (the last one on the lower bar).

10. Choose a photo from the library or take a new one, choose the size, and when it has loaded click on it to display it. Then click the **Send** button (in the bottom right-hand corner) and select the **Below Content** option.

11. Go back to the editor and, to introduce a quote, click the **Quote** button and type its text where you find the cursor.

12. When you have completed the post, click the **Done** button on the keyboard and then the **Editor's Publish** button. Check the result on your blog.

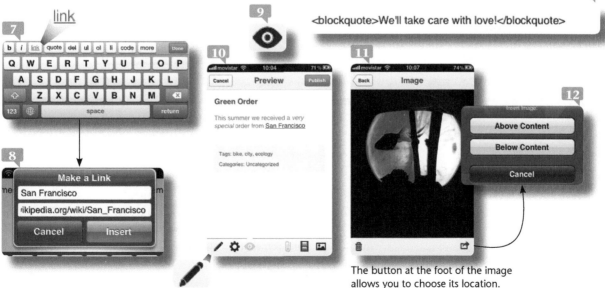

The button at the foot of the image allows you to choose its location.

Managing comments from an iPhone

AS FAR AS MANAGING COMMENTS GOES, WordPress.com's mobile applications are very useful. The Comments screen gathers all of the blog's comments, allows them to be moderated one-by-one or as a group, and also allows you to respond immediately.

1. You will be working with an iPhone again, but you can adapt the exercise to any other device, provided that it has the Word-Press.com application. On your mobile device, activate the **Comments** screen from the main menu by selecting its tab. **1**

2. This screen gathers your blog's comments classified as **Pending moderation** and **Comments** (these are the ones that have already been published). **2** If you press on one of them, it will open on the screen.

3. You are shown who the user is (in this case the user is called **Grateful**), then the date and the post to which it belongs, and, finally, the comment itself. **3** On the button bar at the bottom of the screen, the first allows you to approve publication, the second allows you to erase it, the third to mark it as **Spam**, the fourth to edit it, **4** and the fifth to reply to it. **5**

4. When you approve a comment, it automatically goes to the **Published Comments** section. You can do several things

The buttons in the top right-hand corner of a screen allow you to see ptrevious or later posts.

134

from the **Comments** page. You must first press the **Edit** button  to display the selection buttons in the posts.

5. Select, for example, those that you would like to mark as **Spam**, and click the button with a flag icon. ⁷

6. You can continue editing and select, for example, those comments you would like to approve and click **Correct**. ⁸

7. Finally, you can erase any message by clicking on the Trash can icon.

8. You can also select a comment that has already been approved and published and send it to the Pending file by clicking on the **Reject** button (the X icon). ⁹ When you have finished editing the comments click **Done**.

9. Click on your mobile device's **Settings** icon ¹⁰ and select the **Notifications** option. ¹¹

10. Click on the name of the application, **WordPress**, ¹² and on your settings screen make sure that you have the **Notification Center** activated and have chosen an alert style. ¹³

11. Select the last options on the screen and enjoy receiving immediate notifications of the comments made on your blog. ¹⁴

Publishing with iPhone's Quick Photo function

WORDPRESS.COM OFFERS OTHER RESOURCES TO MAKE sharing information with other users increasingly easier. In this exercise you will learn how tu use the quick publication option for images in iOS that practically makes taking a photograph and publishing it a single action.

1. The WordPress mobile application has a function called **Quick Photo** that allows you to publish a standard format image extremely quickly. To open it, press the **Photo** button in the WordPress for iOS application.

2. Although you can load an image from your mobile, you can choose between taking a new photograph or using one from the library, we think that Quick Photo makes more sense when you want to take a photo and publish it immediately.

3. Just select the desired option, take the photograph, and press the **Use** button, or if you wish to select one from your gallery, simply select its thumbnail.

You can access the Quick Photo function with the button that displays the text Photo in the WordPress for iOS menu.

4. A simple post editing screen opens where you can see the loaded image. **4** Type a title and descriptive text. **5**

5. When you have finished, simply press **Publish**, which is the button on the top right-hand corner of the screen.

6. The content will be published in a new post after it has been loaded onto the server. When the process is finished (and the **Quick Photo** button is reactivated), access your blog to check that the image has been published automatically. **6**

7. Open the post in WordPress.com to check its appearance. **7** Note that the photograph has been inserted at the maximum size and that neither a category nor a tag has been assigned to it. It would be best to edit the post from WordPress.com or from your mobile, when you have a moment, to add these details that make browsing easy for users. Go to the Posts screen from the menu in WordPress for iOS and select the post that you created with the **Quick Photo** function.

8. Assign tags and categories to it. **8**

9. In the content, change the following text: **alignnone size-full** **9** to: **alingcenter width=300** **10** and update it.

IMPORTANT

The Reader button on the WordPress for iOS application's Dashboard (to the left of the Photo button) allows you to access a handy blog reader.

In the same way, you can align to the right (alignright), to the left (alignleft), and define any width (width) or height (height).

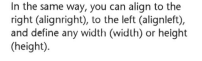

A post published with the Quick Photo function has exactly the same appearance as any other post.

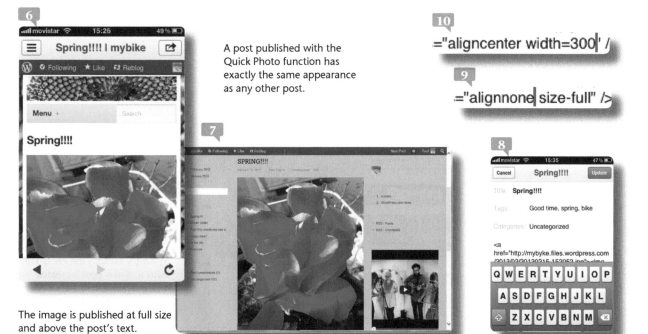

The image is published at full size and above the post's text.

Press This or creating posts with a click

YOU CAN ADD A TOOL TO your bookmarks bar that allows you to create posts from other websites. Without having to enter WordPress.com you can directly insert text, images, and links, modify these texts and publish posts.

1. In this exercise you will learn about another tool designed to allow quick publishing on your WordPress.com blog. Open your Dashboard on WordPress.com.

2. Click the **Tools** tab 🔲 to go to its screen.

3. The first section, **Press This**, explains what the **Press This** tool does. 🔲 Drag and drop the link to your browser's bookmarks bar. 🔲

4. You will now learn how to create a post without needing to access WordPress.com. Open a website in you browser that might have some information relevant to your blog. When you have found an interesting page, click the **Press This** button. 🔲

To insert the tool, make sure that the bookmarks bar is visible, and drag and drop the icon for it.

By simply clicking the **Press This** button, a new post is created into which a link to the website you are visiting is inserted.

5. A window opens with a new post, and in the body text a link to the website is automatically inserted. 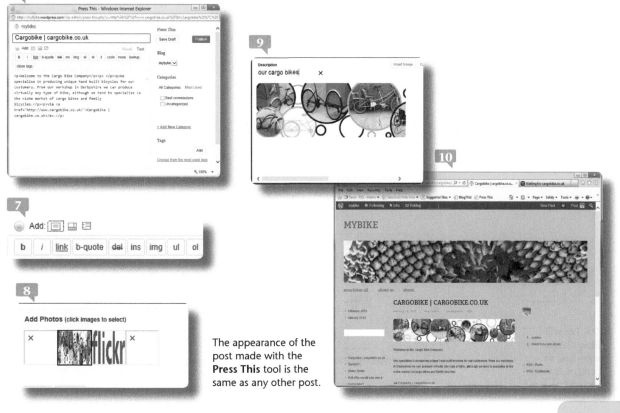 Click the **Save Draft** button.

6. This way, you will be able to return to the draft later to use the link in a post. Close the editor.

7. Select a fragment of text from the website you are visiting and click the **Press This** button in your bookmarks bar again.

8. By doing this, the selected text is pasted into a new post, the source is cited, and a link to it is created. Click the **Insert an Image** button that is above the toolbar.

9. A panel expands that allows you to choose from the images in the page you are visiting. Select one by clicking on it.

10. In the new window that opens, type a description into the correct field and click the **Insert Image** button.

11. The image is inserted into the post's header. You can select it and modify its size or add categories and tags, among many other things. Publish the post and click the **View Post** link to check the result.

063

IMPORTANT

If you have various blogs in your account, the **Press This** module (in the box of the same name) allows you to choose which of them you would like to publish the post in.

The appearance of the post made with the **Press This** tool is the same as any other post.

Publishing by e-mail

IMPORTANT

Do not disclose your WordPress.com secret address to anybody unless you want to allow them to publish on your blog. Be aware that any message sent to this address, regardless of who has sent it, will be published as a post immediately.

THE PUBLISH BY E-MAIL TOOL ALLOWS you to publish a post from any e-mail service and from any account. You will need to obtain a secret address that, in this case, will be generated by WordPress.com, to which you should send the content that you would like to publish.

1. You will work with another tool created for making publishing posts easy. On your blog's Dashboard, click the **Dashboard** tab and then click **My Blogs** in the secondary tab.

2. Were you to have various blogs, they would all appear on this page where you would be able to complete different managing actions. If you were to click on a blog's name, you would access its Dashboard, but were you to click on its address, you would access the blog.

3. Place the pointer over the address to display its options: the first allows you to change your blog's address, and the second allows you to transfer your blog to another user. When you apply this option you will lose your status as administrator for the blog permanently.

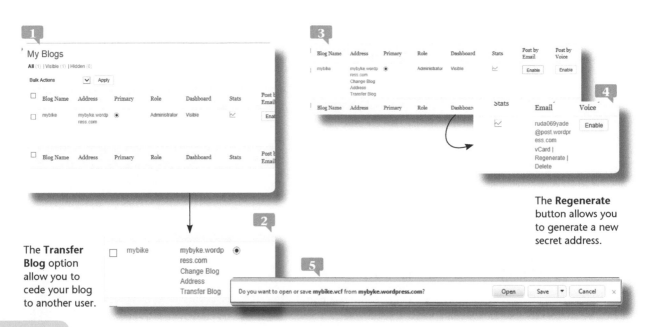

The **Transfer Blog** option allow you to cede your blog to another user.

The **Regenerate** button allows you to generate a new secret address.

4. Now click on the **Enable** button in the **Post by E-mail** column. 3

5. A secret e-mail address is generated for publishing your posts by e-mail. Place the pointer over it to display its options.

6. Click on the **VCard** option 4 and, in the dialog box that opens, make sure that your instant messaging service is enabled and click **Open**. 5

7. The address is now available in your e-mail's contact list manager. 6 You can also store the file and import it to your e-mail service. If this is Gmail, you need only access your Contacts page, 7 click on the **More** button, and select the **Import** option. 8

8. Now click the **Browse** button, select the file that was previously exported, and click **Import** to be able to see it on your contact list.

9. Should you wish to publish a message by e-mail, you should send it to the supplied address. Remember that the subject will become the title of the message, that the message body will become the post's text, and that applied styles will be maintained when possible, although you might find some unexpected results. Why don't you test it out from your mobile 10 and check the result? 11

Configuring publication by e-mail

IF YOU WOULD LIKE TO PUBLISH posts from e-mail messages, you might want to apply tags or categories, customize the way in which images are shown, or create a gallery or a slideshow. In this exercise, you will learn how to do this by using some simple codes.

1. If you would like to have total control over the appearance of posts published through e-mail, you will need to learn some simple codes. In this exercise you will work with some of them. Create a new e-mail message to be sent to your own secret address.

2. Attach a selection of photographs to the message and, to store them in your blog's library without publishing them, send it to your secret address, but in this case write the text **media+** in front of it. For example: media+YOUR_SECRET_ADDRESS. 🗨

3. Go to your **Media Library** 🗨 in WordPress.com and see how all the images that were sent by e-mail appear in the **Unattached** category. 🗨

4. Create a new e-mail addressed to your secret address, attach various images (you can use the same ones), and insert a title and text.

media+ruda069yade@post.wordpress.com

To send images to your WordPress.com account without publishing them, send an e-mail to media+YOUR_SECRET_ADDRESS.

You will find the sent files in your blog's Media Library.

5. At the bottom of the post, introduce the following codes. Substitute the capital letters for the concepts they identify.

   [category POST CATEGORY]

   [excerpt]EXCERPT FROM THE POST.[/excerpt]

   [tags LABEL1, LABEL2, LABEL3]

   [status draft]

   [geotag on]

   [end] 🔳

6. The code [status draft] means that the post will be stored as a draft, [geotag on] activates the geo-localization for the post, and [end] indicates where the post ends and omits any later text such as signatures. Send the e-mail message, and on your **WordPress.com** Dashboard, go to the **Posts** screen.

7. You can now see that your post is identified as a draft. 🔳 Display its options and select the one called **Preview**.

   Check the result. Both categories as well as tags are displayed, and the photographs are organized in a gallery. 🔳 You can also use the following codes in your e-mails: [slideshow] for creating a slideshow rather than a gallery, [nogallery] to display the photographs inserted into the text, [more] to insert a break on the front page and the **More** label, [comments on | off] to activate or deactivate comments, and [delay +1 hour] to set the publication of the post in an hour, or +1 day to set publication for the next day.

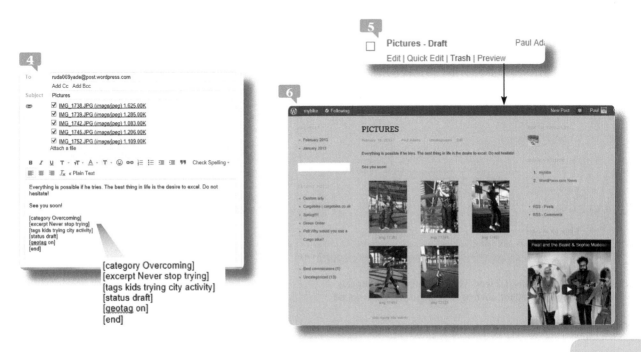

Controlling writing and reading settings

IN WORDPRESS.COM'S SETTINGS SECTION YOU WILL find settings options for each element in your blog and its associated services. In this exercise you will work with the Writing and Reading settings for customizing some of the default functions.

1. Click the **Settings** tab, which is at the bottom of your WordPress.com website.

2. Click the secondary tab **Writing** to display its **Settings** options.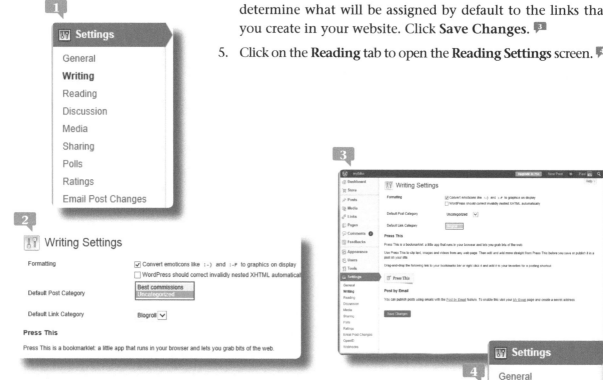

3. In this section, you can set emoticons to be substituted for their graphic equivalents and for automatically correcting XHTML nesting errors. Expand the **Default Post Category** menu and choose the most suitable option for your blog.

4. The next field called **Default Link Category** allows you to determine what will be assigned by default to the links that you create in your website. Click **Save Changes**.

5. Click on the **Reading** tab to open the **Reading Settings** screen.

In the **Writing Settings** screen, you can define some aspects of your blog's text editor, such as the category to be assigned by default.

066

6. Modify the maximum number of posts to be shown on the blog's front page. In the next field define how many are to appear in the feed. 🔲5

7. You can also define whether the feed will display the complete text of each post or only excerpts. The **Scroll Infinitely** option allows the blog to recharge automatically, **To infinity and beyond,** with the oldest posts, without needing to click the traditional **Older Posts** link when a reader reaches the bottom of the page. This option is activated by default, but can be deactivated by selecting its check box. 🔲6

8. In the **Enhanced Feeds** section, you can decide which elements should be included in the feed. Select the objects you want. 🔲7

9. The next section, **Follower Settings**, defines the communication with the blog's followers. The first option allows you to decide whether the **Follow** button will be displayed to users who have not yet logged in. Select the option you prefer.

10. The text typed into the **Blog follow e-mail text** field is the one that will be shown to users who click your blog's **Follow** button. The next one is the text that will be received by users who follow the comments on a particular post. Modify both with suitable text for your blog. 🔲8 Click **Save Changes**.

5

Reading Settings

Front page displays	◉ Your latest posts
	○ A static page (select below)
	Front page: Why MyBike ▾
	Posts page: About ▾
Blog pages show at most	10 posts
Syndication feeds show the most recent	10 items

Do not forget to customize the text that will be sent automatically to users when they click the Follow button of either the blog or of a particular post.

Changes may not appear until you create a new post or your news reader refreshes.

6

| To infinity and beyond | ☑ Scroll Infinitely |
| | (Shows 7 posts on each load) |

7

Enhanced Feeds

Add to each article in your feed:	☑ Categories
	☑ Tags
	☑ Comment count
	☑ Sharing

Follower Settings

These settings change emails sent from your blog to followers.

Logged out users	☑ Show follow button to logged out users.
	Checking this will present a follow button to logged out users in the bottom corner of their screen.
Blog follow email text	Howdy.
	You recently signed up to follow this blog's posts. This means once you confirm below, you will receive each new post by email.
	Introduction text sent when someone follows your blog. (Site and confirmation details will be automatically added for you.)
Comment follow email text	Howdy.
	You recently signed up to follow one of my posts. This means once you confirm below, you will receive an email when new comments are posted.
	Introduction text sent when someone follows a post on your blog. (Site and confirmation details will be automatically added for you.)

Save Changes

Inviting other users

WORDPRESS.COM ALLOWS YOU TO SEND INVITATIONS to users and to offer them up to five different types of permissionst: administrator, editor, author, contributor, and follower. In this exercise you will learn how to do this and will get to know the difference between the various options.

1. If you would like someone else to be able to write in your blog, you must invite them to be a collaborator, author, editor, or administrator. To do so, click on the **Users** tab.

2. In the **All** users screen, you will appear as the only user with the role of administrator. Click the **Invite New** link at the top of the page. 🔳

3. The **Followers** role is selected by default, which invites other users to visit your blog without giving them any other privilege. You can type various e-mail addresses or WordPress users, separated by a comma, and modify the text message. 🔳 Do so and click the **Send Invitation** button.

4. You will see that the text has been sent in the header of the page, 🔳 and at the bottom, in the **Past Invitations** section, 🔳

Invite New

1

2

cathy.bates@gmail.com

Invite up to 10 email addresses and/or WordPress.com usernames, separate a username will be sent instructions on how to create one.

Follower ⌄   *Learn more about roles*

Paul Adams invites you to follow mybike:

I invite you to visit my blog

3

Invite New Users to Your Blog

Invitation(s) sent.

4

Invitee	Sent By	Role	Dat
sllena6@gmail.com	pauladams927	Follower	Feb 3:33
cathy.bates@gmail.com	pauladams927	Follower	Feb 3:32
Invitee	Sent By	Role	Dat

In the **Past Invitations** section of the Invite New Users to Your Blog screen, a list is created of all the sent invitations.

information on all of the invitations that have been sent until now is stored. Expand the **Role** menu.

067

5. Users with the role of **administrator** have complete and un-limited power over the blog. They can even delete the blog at any moment. They are true owners of the blog. An **editor** can see, edit, erase, and publish posts and pages; modify tags, categories, and links; moderate comments; and upload files. An **author** can see, edit, erase, and publish only his or her own posts and pages, as well as files that he or she uploaded. Finally, **contributors** can create and edit their own posts and then submit them for approval by an administrator, who will be the one who publishes them. Once the post has been pub-lished by the administrator, the collaborator can neither edit nor erase it.

6. Once you have sent invitations, you can manage them in the **Past Invitations** section. You can resend them by clicking the **Resend** link in the **Actions** column or erase them with the **Delete** link.

7. Each user will receive an invitation e-mail. If permission has been given, the type will be indicated.

8. When a user receives the invitation, it will be indicated in this column, by displaying the text, **Accepted**.

Each invitation includes an automatically generated message that defines the role of the user and accompanies the text written in the Message field.

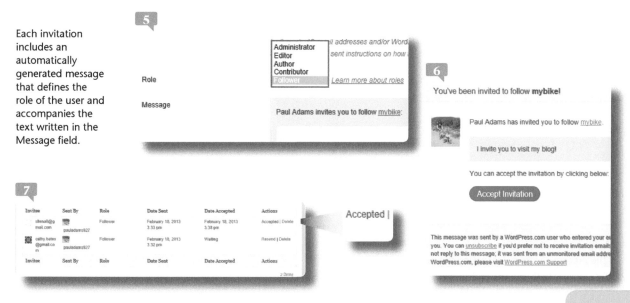

Managing contributors' messages

WHEN CONTRIBUTORS CREATE A POST, THEY cannot add images or other files, but should submit them for approval. One of the editors should open the posts, make any necessary alterations, and publish them.

1. In this exercise, you will pretend that you have contributors on your blog. If you can, send an invitation as contributors to other users or to one of your other e-mail addresses.

2. The invited users receive an e-mail in which they are told that they have been invited to contribute to the blog as a creator and editor of their own posts, but that they will need an editor to publish them.

3. When users click the **Accept Invitation** button, they are sent to the WordPress.com home screen. When they log in (and sign up to the service if they had not already done so) they are invited to set up their own profile.

4. When contributors create a new post, they can type text and assign tags, but they cannot upload files. In fact, these tools are not available in their editor and if they click the **Set Featured Image** link, a message will appear that informs

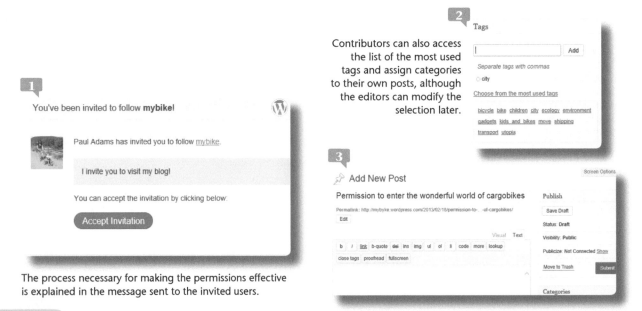

Contributors can also access the list of the most used tags and assign categories to their own posts, although the editors can modify the selection later.

The process necessary for making the permissions effective is explained in the message sent to the invited users.

them that they do not have permission to do so. In the **Publish** panel they have the following options: **Draft** and **Submit for Review**. The latter is to be used once as post is ready.

5. The administrator will find the post written by the contributors in the **All Posts** folder classified as **Pending**. He or She will need to open the post in the editor, select the **Edit** option, and they will be able to add photographs and links, modify categories and tags, and can even change the selected author in the module of the same name. The administrator can finally publish the post.

6. The author's name is displayed in the post's header, and the author's avatar is added in the **Author Grid** widget.

7. When the pointer is placed over the avatar, a profile summary is displayed. When the **View Complete Profile** option is clicked, the profile is displayed in the gravatar.

8. If you would like to change a user's profile, you do not need to send a new invitation. On the **Users** page click the user's check box, expand the menu that displays the profile, select the desired profile, and click the **Change** button. The change is effective immediately, but you should send a notification to the user.

IMPORTANT

If you use the Authors widget instead of the Author Grid widget, the authors' names will be displayed next to their gravatar images.

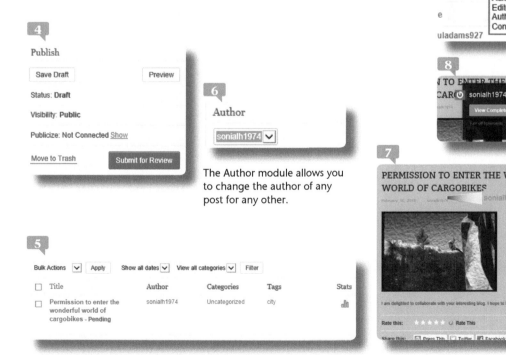

4

Publish

| Save Draft | | Preview |

Status: **Draft**

Visibility: **Public**

Publicize: Not Connected Show

Move to Trash | Submit for Review

6

Author

soníalh1974 ▼

The Author module allows you to change the author of any post for any other.

5

| Bulk Actions ▼ | Apply | Show all dates ▼ | View all categories ▼ | Filter |

	Title	Author	Categories	Tags	Stats
☐	Permission to enter the wonderful world of cargobikes - Pending	sonialh1974	Uncategorized	city	

Analyzing statistics (I)

WORDPRESS.COM OFFERS A WEALTH OF INFORMATION about the traffic on your website that would be useful to know and analyze to improve its weak points and optimize its strengths. Although at the moment of this book's publication they are still accessible from your blog's Dashboard, WordPress.com has announced that they will be transferred completely to the WordPress.com Dashboard.

1. Click the **Dashboard** tab from your blog's website.

2. In the **Site Stats** module there is a complete graph that displays the statistics of your site's recent visits. Below this, the **Top Posts & Pages** column shows the most popular posts and pages visited today and yesterday. 🔳 If you click on the name of any post, this will be displayed on screen. Place the pointer over one of the columns.

3. The column is highlighted and the corresponding date, the number of visits for this day, and the published posts are shown in a floating tag. 🔳 Click it.

4. You are sent to the statistics page for this day on your WordPress.com Dashboard. The header shows the date and

Top Posts & Pages

| Today | Yesterday | | Summaries |

No top posts or pages. This panel shows your most viewed posts and pages.

the number of visits, and the **Referrers** panel shows the links used by people to access the site on the day in question. ▶3 If the site was accessed via a search engine, when you click on the arrowhead icon, a field expands to show which one it was. The **Search Engine Terms** module indicates the keywords used in search engines to access the blog, ▶4 **Top Post & Pages** indicates the content of the greatest amount of traffic, and **Clicks** indicates the links on your site clicked by the users to visit other sites on that day. ▶5 Click the **Return to Stats** link.

5. A bar graph that shows the day-by-day visits is displayed again. ▶6 Click the **Summaries** link.

6. Visits for months and years, average per Day, and Recent Weeks are displayed. ▶7 At the bottom of this page you will find an interesting text about the analytics in tables. ▶8 Click the **Return to Stats** link.

7. You can also access the summaries of the statistics of the most visited content, references used for accessing the website, keywords used in external search engines, and clicks on the blog's links. You can also check the most visited tags and categories, as well as other things that you will analyze in the next lesson.

5

Clicks

Your visitors clicked these links on your site.

2013-01-30

URL	Clicks
nourishesall.blogspot.com.es	1
Total clicks on links on your blog	1

6

📊 February 19, 2013, 2:30 pm

Did you know you can view enhanced stats on the WordPress.com homepage? Check it out now *Now with 100% more visitor stats!*

Days Weeks Months

Summaries

You can modify the time filter in each module.

7

📊 February 19, 2013, 2:38 pm
« Return to Stats

Months and Years

	Jan	Feb	Mar	Apr	May	Jun	Jul	Aug	Sep	Oct	Nov	Dec	Total
2013	28	11											39

Average per Day

	Jan	Feb	Mar	Apr	May	Jun	Jul	Aug	Sep	Oct	Nov	Dec	Overall
2013	2	1											1

Recent Weeks

Mon	Tue	Wed	Thu	Fri	Sat	Sun	Total	Average	Change
Jan 14	Jan 15	Jan 16	Jan 17	Jan 18	Jan 19	Jan 20			
			2	4			6	1	
Jan 21	Jan 22	Jan 23	Jan 24	Jan 25	Jan 26	Jan 27			
	1						1	0	-83.33%
Jan 28	Jan 29	Jan 30	Jan 31	Feb 1	Feb 2	Feb 3			
11		8					19	3	+1,000.00%
Feb 4	Feb 5	Feb 6	Feb 7	Feb 8	Feb 9	Feb 10			

8

About the math

If you try to verify our computations using the numbers in these tables you might get different results. The logic is explained here.

An average is the sum of views divided by the number of days.

We exclude days prior to the first recorded view and future days.

Today (Feb 19) is excluded from averages because it isn't over yet.

Yearly averages are computed from sums, not an average of monthly averages.

Averages are rounded to the nearest integer for display.

Gray zeroes are exactly zero. Black zeroes have been rounded down.

Percent change is computed from weekly averages before they are rounded.

Analyzing statistics (II)

WORDPRESS.COM'S STATISTICS ARE SO DETAILED THAT you can find out which authors generate the most traffic, which users make the most comments, or which posts have the most comments, among other things.

1. You can minimize any of WordPress.com's statistics modules by clicking on the **Minus** (-) sign in the top right-hand corner. Try it.

2. The **Totals, Followers & Shares** panel gives you a summarized view of your blog. In its **Content** section, the number of posts you have is displayed without counting pages and comments. Under the **Content** section the number of tags and categories used in your blog is indicated, and in **Followers** the number of followers and followers of comments is displayed. Click the **Blog** link in this category. 🗨

3. A new window opens that displays your blog's followers with their avatars. Click the **Email Followers** tab. 🗨

4. The e-mail addresses of those users who have asked to receive new posts by e-mail is displayed. 🗨 Click the **Site Stats** link

The **Totals, Followers & Shares** module also displays information on the number of times your blog has been shared (the Share tab), as well as information about the spam that has been filtered, whether it be manually or with Akismet (WordPress's automatic filter).

○ Blog

1

Totals, Followers & Shares

Totals Shares Spam

Content

15
≡ Posts

2
☰ Categories

13
✐ Tags

Followers (includes Publicize)

2
○ Blog

0
○ Comments

2

Site Stats » My Followers (2)

WordPress.com Followers (1) | Email Followers (1)

	WordPress.com User	Following
	Paul Adams	1 month ag
	http://mybike.wordpress.com	
	WordPress.com User	Following

3

Site Stats » My Followers (2)

WordPress.com Followers (1) | **Email Followers** (1)

	Email Address	Following
	sliena6@gmail.com	23 hours, 2
	Email Address	Following

to return to the previous page and then click the **Comments** link to see the details.

5. You can find out the number of followers each post has, but not who they are. 🔲 Go back to the **Site Stats** page.

6. If your blog has various authors, the **Top Authors** module shows the authors who receive the most visits and the number of visits they have received in the period analyzed. Finally, the **Comments** module shows the user who has made the most comments on your blog recently. 🔲 If you click on one of the names, you will be sent to your blog's **Comments** screen, where all of that particular user's comments are shown. 🔲 Go back to the previous page.

7. Still in the **Comments** panel, click the **Most Commented** tab.

8. The posts with the most comments are displayed. 🔲 If you click on the title of one of them, the post will open on the screen. 🔲 Click the **Summary** tab.

9. The most relevant information on the comments statistics is displayed in the same panel.

Anonymous users and those who have not identified themselves with an e-mail address will not be counted in the **Top Recent Commenters** column.

If your blog has various authors, it is important to know which of them attract the most traffic.

Migrating from Blogger to WordPress.com

IF YOU HAVE CREATED YOUR BLOG in Blogger, it is likely that the time will come when you will find it somewhat "small." This would be the moment to migrate it to WordPress.com. You will learn how to export your blog from Blogger and import it into WordPress.com.

1. Let us imagine that you have a blog that was created in Blogger that you would like to migrate to WordPress.com. You will obviously first need to access your Blogger Dashboard and by the blog you would like to migrate. Do so now, click the **Settings** tab and then click the secondary tab called **Other**.

2. In the **Blog Tools** section you have the **Import blog**, **Export blog**, and **Delete blog** links. Click the **Export blog** button.

3. A dialog box opens that informs you that the blog will be exported to the **Atom** format. Click the **Download Blog** button and in the following dialog box, confirm that you would like to save the file.

4. Go to your WordPress.com Dashboard, click the **My Blogs** secondary tab (in **Dashboard**), and click on the **Register Another Blog** button.

Before importing the XML file, you should create the blog to which you will import it.

5. Insert the requested details for the new blog.

6. Choose and apply a suitable theme.

7. When the WordPress.com website welcomes you, click on the **My Blogs** tab and click the **Dashboard** link that corresponds to the new blog. 🔲

8. When you enter the new blog's **Dashboard**, click the **Tools** tab and then the **Import** secondary tab. 🔲

9. You can import posts and other content from various services. Blogger is at the top. Click this option. 🔲

10. You are sent to the **Import Blogger** screen. Click the **Browse** button in the **Have a Blogger export file?** section at the bottom of the page, 🔲 find the XML file and click the **Upload File and Import** button.

11. You will be told that the file has been successfully uploaded and that it is now being processed. When complete you will be able to see your posts on the **All Posts** screen. 🔲 Blogger does not assign tags and often, when the import is being processed, the tags are interpreted as categories in WordPress.com. In the next exercise you will see how to correct this. Go to the blog created to check the result. 🔲

12. Maybe you do not like the appearance of the blog's pages, but posts, photographs, the majority of the videos (those from YouTube, Vimeo, and Blip), and the comments have been imported correctly. 🔲

7

mybike

Clearly Paul

Create a New Blog

8 | Tools

Available Tools
Import
Delete Site
Export

9 Blogger

10

Have a Blogger export file?

To fetch your export file, go to Settings -> Export blog in the control panel for your Blogger blog.

Choose a file from your computer: (Maximum size: 15MB)   Browse...

Once the importing process has finished, you will be able to see your Blogger posts on the corresponding screen of your new blog.

When you import a blog, you will keep videos embedded from YouTube, but not the ones from Google Videos (which no longer exists), or those imported directly from Blogger.

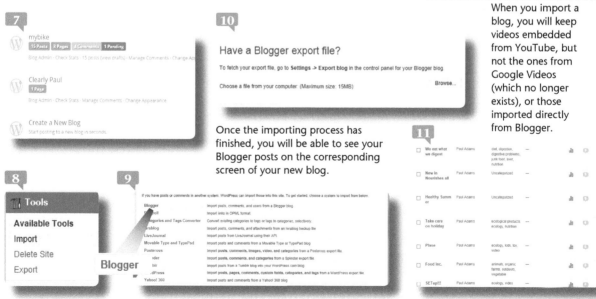

Importing a blog directly from Blogger

YOU CAN ALSO IMPORT A FILE from Blogger directly to another from WordPress.com and, in this case, you can also manage the authors. Later on, you can convert the categories back into tags by using another WordPress.com tool.

1. Create a third test blog in WordPress.com by following the process that you already know. Go to the Dashboard of this third WordPress.com blog.

2. Before going ahead with the import, display the **All Posts** screen and erase the post that was created by default as well as the blog's sample page.

3. Just as you did in the previous exercise, go to the **Import** screen in the **Tools** section.

4. Click on the first option, Blogger, and, this time, click the first button, **Authorize** on the **Import Blogger** page. If you have not already logged into a Google service, you will be asked to do so now.

5. Once the session has begun, authorize access by WordPres.com to your Blogger account by clicking on the **Grant Access** button.

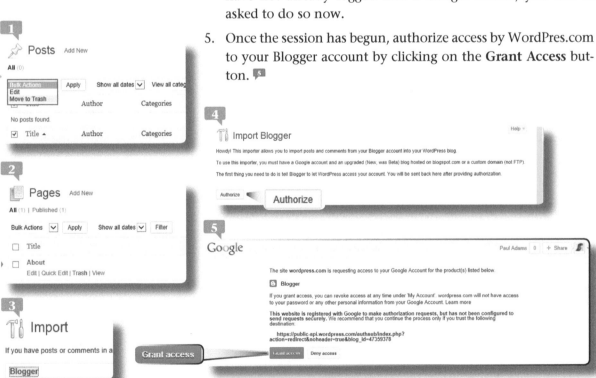

6. The **Blogger Blogs** screen is displayed, which shows all of your blogs on this service. Click the **Import** button from the blog you would like to migrate to WordPress.com, and wait until the process is complete.

7. Go to your inbox and check that they have been imported. If they have not, wait a little longer.

8. As in the previous exercise, the tags have been converted into categories and you have lost the videos that you uploaded directly to Blogger. It would be best to load them now in You-Tube and re-embed them into the new blog.

9. Let us deal with the tags. Click the Import button in the Tools section on the Dashboard of your new WordPress.com blog and click the **Categories and Tags Converter** link.

10. Select the categories that you would like to convert back into tags and click the **Convert Categories to Tags** button.

11. When the process is finished, you will receive an e-mail to confirm completion. Go to the **Tags** screen in **Posts** and check that the change has been made. Click the **Import** secondary tab again and click on **Blogger**.

12. Click the **Set Authors** button of the imported blog.

13. On the **Author Mapping** page, indicate which author will be assigned to each of the Blogger author's posts. When you have finished, click the **Save Changes** button.

IMPORTANT

It is advisable to erase your Blogger blog once you have migrated it, as Google searches penalize duplicated Internet content. To do so, click the **Delete Blog** option in **Settings** and **Other** on your blog's Blogger Dashboard.

6

Blogger Blogs

Screen Options ▾   Help ▾

Blog Name	Blog URL	Posts	Comments	
Nourishes all	nourishesall.blogspot.com	0 of 9	0 of 5	Import

Import Information

8

☑ ecological products (1)
☐ ecology (4)
☐ holidays (1)
☑ junk food (1)
☑ kids (2)
☐ liver (1)
☑ nutrition (3)
☐ organic farms (1)
☐ outdoors (1)
☑ toy (1)
☐ Uncategorized (2)
☐ vegetable (1)
☐ video (2)
☐ Xmas (1)

[Convert Categories to Tags]

7

Categories and Tags Converter

9

Comments

| 5 of 5 | Set Authors |

10

Nourishes all (nourishesall.blogspot.com)

All posts were imported with the current user as author. Use this form to move each Blogger user's posts to a users and then return to this page and complete the user mapping. This form may be used as many times as function below.

Blogger username	WordPress login
Paul Adams	Paul Adams ▾
Sonia	Paul Adams ▾

[Save Changes]

If you would like to transfer all of the authors, you must first register them as users on your blog with the relevant permissions.

Creating a Twitter profile

TODAY, TWITTER IS THE PREEMINENT MICROBLOGGING tool. It is a social network based on the interchange (usually in real time) of short messages called tweets, which are no longer than 140 characters. It has revolutionized, once again, the world of communication.

1. Enter the **www.twitter.com** website and fill out the necessary data for setting up your account, if you do not already have one. **1**

2. On the next page, **Join Twitter Today**, you will receive feedback on all the data that you have submitted, and a username is suggested for your Twitter account. **2** If you would like to modify it, click the **Create my account** button. **3**

3. To complete the process you must access the e-mail account that you supplied and open an e-mail that has been sent by Twitter. Confirm your account by clicking on the relevant button. **4**

4. You are sent back to Twitter and a message informs you that your account has been confirmed. **5**

IMPORTANT

When this book was written, there were over 465 million Twitter accounts worldwide. Eleven Twitter accounts were created per second and 11 million accounts were created per day. Four thousand tweets were sent per second, and 175 million tweets were sent per day.

158

5. Before starting to tweet, it is advisable to set up your profile. Click on your name ⬛ to access your profile page (your introduction on Twitter).

6. It is empty for the moment. Click the **Edit** button. ⬛

7. As with all social networks, you should assign a photograph of yourself or an image that represents and identifies you. If the user is a corporation, it is important that this image is clearly recognizable by using your logo or an adequate adaptation of it. You can upload a profile photo of up to 700 kb in JPG, GIF, or PNG formats. If you do not have one, prepare one now in Photoshop and, when it is ready, click the **Change Photo** button and upload it. ⬛

8. Indicate the URL of your website or blog in the next field.

9. Its **Location** is of great importance if you would like to use the account professionally. Provide it now.

10. The **biography** should be clear, attractive, and descriptive. It should also include words that help to identify it as well as the mission of the user. ⬛

11. You would surely like to **share** your tweets on Facebook and other websites, but we will leave this for later. For the moment, click the **Save Changes** button.

IMPORTANT

In this example we have created a profile for an individual, but you could also do so for your business. Although Twitter is used mainly at a personal level, it is increasingly used by businesses and organizations as a channel for exchanging information with clients and suppliers, etc.

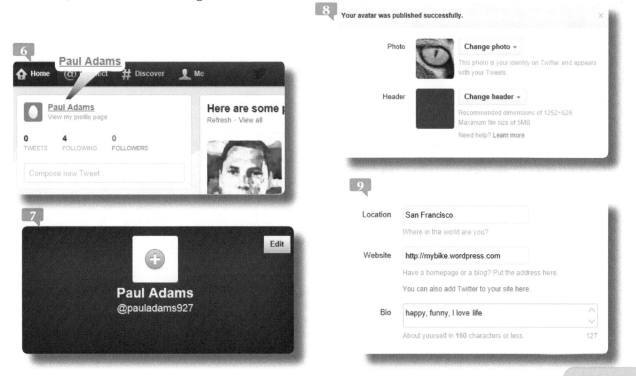

Customizing Twitter's profile template

TWITTER ALLOWS YOU TO CHANGE YOUR profile photo as well as the background and the colors of the themes. With the Themeleon online application, you can use an extensive selection of colors, themes, and completely customizable templates.

1. Click on the **Design** tab on your profile page. **1**

2. Even though you can now select a pre-made theme, click the **Check out Themeleon** link. **2**

3. Themeleon is an extremely versatile template designer. Click the **Sign in** **3** button and allow the application to access your details on Twitter.

4. The preview is updated and now your profile is displayed. The **Themes** section **4** allows you to apply a theme with a background image. Use the arrowhead buttons on either side of the Themes bar to view all the samples and apply one that you like.

5. In the **Background** section, click the **Patterns** tab, select a template, and see what happens.

6. At the bottom of the enlarged view of the pattern, you will find samples of each color in which the pattern is available. Click one of them. **5**

Themeleon offers you a high level of customization for your profile, allowing you to stand out and to become recognizable.

074

7. A palette opens that allows you to create a new color to re-place the previous one.  Customize the pattern's colors.

8. Try out different options in the **Layout** module, check its effect on your profile with the preview, and apply one that you like.

9. You can also use one of your own photographs as a back-ground for your profile. In the **Background** section, click the **Images** tab, click the **Browse** button, double-click on the cho-sen image, and then click the **Upload** button.

10. Hide the editor by clicking the **Hide** button at the bottom to check the effect on the profile. If you are happy with the result, click the **Save Profile** button. If not, click **Show** and use the **Undo** button, which is between the **Background** and **Layout** modules.

11. You are now offered the possibility of creating a profile with COLOURlovers, which is a type of social network in which the users share all sorts of color and theme palettes. They are classified in different categories that allow you to keep a record of your designs, create a favorites folder, and access some cre-ative tools, amongst which is Themeleon itself. For now, just click **No thanks, take me to my profile** to finish.

IMPORTANT

In the **Patterns** module of the Themeleon template designer, there are four buttons to the right of the enlarged view of the pattern. The first, **Undo**, allows you to return to previously applied options, the second randomly introduces colors from the page design, the third applies the colors from the page design into the pattern, and the fourth applies the colors of the pattern into the page design.

Following on Twitter

ONCE YOU HAVE CREATED YOUR OWN profile on Twitter, the next step is to follow other users. In this exercise we will give you some clues about how to find tweets of interest.

1. To begin to build a network on Twitter, click the **# Discover** tab in the header.

2. This page is made to help you find information of interest to you. The **Tweets** panel displays a selection of the hottest recent topics on Twitter, and each one displays avatars of the users who have tweeted it. Click on one to display its **Profile summary**.

3. If you click the **Follow** button, you will receive all of their new tweets. Close it and now click the **Who to follow** tab.

4. Here you will find a selection of users. Type into the field provided the name or e-mail address of someone you would like to find and click the **Search Twitter** button. When you have found someone who interests you, click the **Follow** menu button.

5. If you click on their name, you can access the profile summary and their most recent tweets. You can then access their full

There are many ways to discover who to follow on Twitter.

profile and read their oldest tweets. **6** Click the button to the left of the **Following** button.

6. From this menu you can tweet it, add it to a list, block it, report it as spam, prevent it from being retweeted, or activate mobile notifications. **7** Click the **Browse Categories** link in the panel on the left.

7. Another way to find interesting accounts to follow is through these different categories that Twitter proposes. Next to each category is the number of suggested users. **8** Click on one of the category titles.

8. Locate, in this way, some contacts that you would like to follow and click the appropriate button for doing so. **9**

9. Type in the search field at the top of the page something you would like to find, even if it no more than a keyword, business, or individual **10** and click the **Tweets** tab.

10. The tweets that include the keywords are displayed. Click the **People** tab in the panel on the left. **11**

11. Users whose name includes the keywords are now displayed.

You can also search for relevant images or videos that have been tweeted.

IMPORTANT

If you click on the **Find Friends** tab, a module expands that allows you to automatically search your e-mail accounts.

When you create a search using the field in the header, a menu is displayed with a quick selection of possible responses.

Tweeting and mentioning

IF YOU ALREADY FOLLOW SOME USERS on Twitter, now is the time to begin to tweet yourself. In this exercise you will learn some tips so that you can tweet like an expert.

1. It is now time to start tweeting, so let's get to work. Click the paper and quill button on the upper right-hand corner.

2. A floating window opens that asks, **"What's happening?"** which is what Twitter users would like to know. Think of something that might be of interest to others and type it.

3. Click **Add Image** (the camera icon), to add an image.

4. Choose a relevant image from your computer and click the **Open** button to upload it.

5. The image will appear in your tweet as a link. Now click the **Add Location** button, which is next to the previous one.

6. A new dialog box with a brief explanation on how it works opens. Click the **Turn location on** button.

You can access the Compose New Tweet button.

You can add an image and its location to a tweet.

Add a location to your Tweets
When you tweet with a location, Twitter stores that location. You can switch location on/off before each Tweet and always have the option to delete your location history. Learn more

7. By default, unless you are using an application that uses precise coordinates, only the city will be indicated, and perhaps just the area. Correct the text, if you wish, and if you would like to insert a URL, type it. Twitter will shorten it to nineteen characters and will display a short link. Once your message is ready, click the **Tweet** button.

8. If you click the **Tweets** tab in your profile, you will see how your first message appears. Click the **View photo** link.

9. This is the full view of your tweet. Click the **Following** link to see all the users who are following it at the moment.

10. The Twitter username preceded by an @ symbol, appears next to each username. Imagine that you would like to say something about one of the users that you follow: copy the Twitter username.

11. Create a new tweet that mentions the selected user, using your username without omitting the @ symbol.

12. When you have entered the profile, click the **Tweets** link again.

13. The reference changes into a link that allows you to access the Profile summary of the user in question. This user has automatically received a notification of your message.

IMPORTANT

If you click the Favorite button of a tweet, it will be saved in your favorite folder, which you can access by clicking on the favorite button in your profile.

★ Favorite

You will recognize the Twitter username because it is preceded by an @ symbol.

When you use a username, Twitter creates a link to its profile at the same time that a notification is received.

Retweeting and using hashtags

IF YOU HAVE READ A TWEET that is worthy of sharing, you can retweet it, provided that you mention the author. In this exercise we will show you how to do so automatically and manually. Furthermore, you can identify your tweets with labels and make searches for those of other users.

1. When you click **Followers** the users who are following you are displayed. It would be appropriate for you to follow them as well. As you know, it is a matter of a simple click. If you would like to be polite, you can type them a thank-you message for following you.

2. Open the menu of any user, you can select the option **Tweet to...** to create a new tweet that automatically refers to them.

3. Type a tweet addressed to this user or that just mentions them: in both cases the message will reach them and, if their profile is public, it can also be seen by any other user who might wish to read it. When you have finished, tweet it.

4. Go the website's home page by clicking its tab.

5. Here, you will find all of your community's latest tweets (yours included). Find a tweet here (or in the profile of another user who interests you) that is worth sharing.

If you block a user, they will not be able to follow you, nor add you to their lists, and their references will not appear on your site.

In the **Recent images** section on the right, the most recent images that you uploaded are displayed.

You can deactivate a user's retweets to receive their tweets only.

6. Place the pointer over the tweet that you would like to share and click the **Retweet** link. 5

7. A dialog box opens that asks you to confirm that you would like to retweet to your followers. Click the **Retweet** button. 6

8. Now go to your profile and click the **Tweets** tab to see the appearance of the **RT** (Retweet). 7

9. You can also create a retweet "by hand." Find a tweet that you like, select it and copy it by typing **Ctrl + C**.

10. Open a blank tweet and paste the content of the clipboard. At the beginning of the text type the initials **RT**, that indicate that this is a retweet, followed by the name of the author. 8

11. You can now add personal text, either at the beginning or at the end of the tweet (this cannot be done if you use the Retweet button). Now tweet it.

12. Open your **Tweets** page and see how, in this case, it maintains its own personal image. 9

13. Open the home page or the profile of a practiced user and find a tweet with a # sign.

14. The sign will be followed by a word, without spaces between them. It might be a combination of words. This is called a hashtag. Hashtags work like tags in a blog. In the header bar, search for this word, exactly as it appears preceded by the # sign.

15. The tweet contains the tag appears. 10 Can you see how useful it is now?

IMPORTANT

You can use a hashtag that already exists for appearing in the searches of other users, or create your own hashtag for connecting your tweets on a particular subject. This makes your followers' searches easier, just like the tags in a blog. Choose it carefully because, if it is successful, it will be used by other users (may it always be to your advantage!) Another piece of advice: never use more than two hashtags in one tweet.

You can always distinguish other people's RTs because the sign that identifies them as such is always displayed.

Retweeting manually allows you to add personal comments.

Responding, creating lists, and using direct messages

YOU CAN GROUP FOLLOWERS (OR NON-FOLLOWERS) in public or private lists. Thus, you can send a direct message to any user, provided that they have a Twitter account.

1. For this exercise you will need either a friend on Twitter to make at least one mention about you, or do so using a trial Twitter user. Click the **Connect** tab in the header of the page. 🗨1

2. In the **Interactions** panel you will find the tweets that have been made by you as well as those made by your followers. 🗨2 Click the **Mentions** tab.

3. You can only see the mentions that have been made about you by other users. Display the options of any tweet and click the **Reply** link. 🗨3

4. A new tweet opens into which a mention to the author of the original tweet has been inserted. Write them a message and tweet it. 🗨4

5. Click on **Me**, in the application's header, and choose the **Lists** option. 🗨5

6. The lists group the users by categories. Click the **Create List** button 🗨6 and, in the dialog box that appears, type a name for your first list.

1

🏠 Home   @ Connect   # Discover

2

Interactions

🐦 ☆Skater Steez☆, Sònia Llena and Heartfilled Vocals !   Feb 24
followed you

🐦 When people follow you to read your tweets, you'll be notified here.

3

Mentions

Sònia Llena @Sonia_Llena   1 min
Thanks to @pauladams927. You are a good friend!!
Expand ← Reply t3 Retweet ★ Favorite ••• More

← Reply

4

Mentions

Sònia Llena @Sonia_Llena   4 mins
Thanks to @pauladams927. You are a good friend!!
Collapse ← Reply t3 Retweet ★ Favorite ••• More

6 53 a.m. - Feb 25, 2013 Details

@Sonia_Llena You're welcome! Our friendship will last forever ;-)|

📷 ♀ ▾ Lerida, Lerida   75   Tweet

When you respond to a tweet you create a conversation.

You can respond to any tweet, even if you are not mentioned in it. Your reply will be available to everyone in the original tweet and in your own profile.

5

Tweets
Following
Followers
Favorites
Lists

078

7. Type a description in the following field and decide if the list will be private (only you will be able to see it), or public (other users will be able to see it). When you have finished, click the **Save list** button. 🗨7

8. Now you are in your list, which is empty for the moment. Use the search field to find a user. 🗨8

9. When you have found the user who you would like to add to your list, expand their menu and select the **Add or remove from lists** option. 🗨9

10. Select the list you would like to add them to in the dialog box that opens, and click the **Create list** button. 🗨10

11. Create the lists that you want and add the users you want by using the same method.

12. If you have made them public, the lists that you create will be available in a module with the same name as your profile. You and your users will be able to click on the name of any list and, for example, see the tweets for each of them.

13. On your profile page, click on the **Direct Messages** button, which shows an envelope. 🗨11

14. A window with the same name opens. Click the **New Message** button.

15. In the first field type a username and in the second, a message of nor more than 140 characters. When you have finished, click the **Send message** button. 🗨12

16. A preview of the sent message is displayed. Close the window to finish.

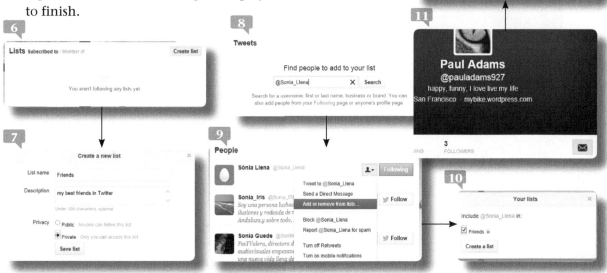

169

Tweeting from your mobile

TWITTER IS A SOCIAL NETWORK THAT lends itself extremely well to being used from a mobile phone. The application for the iPhone has very similar structure to that of the website and features almost all of the same functions.

1. For this exercise, download the Twitter application on your smartphone. In Twitter's help center, **https://support.twitter.com/**, you can find more information about the appropriate application for your device. You will be working with Twitter for iPhone.

2. Open the application by clicking on its icon and allow it to use your location, at least for the moment. ▪

3. Press the button on the home page. ▪

4. Now insert your Twitter username and your password, and press the **Sign in** button again. ▪

5. Permit notifications from the application.

6. Just as when you create a user on the web, the application offers to search for Twitter users among your mobile phone contacts. ▪ Remember that you will only be able to see those users who have associated their account with their mobile number. To select a contact, press the + sign Twitter icon (to the right of their name). ▪

7. When you have finished searching for new contacts, click the **Finish** button.

8. Access your timeline. Press the **Compose New Tweet** button that is identical to the one on the website.

9. The application's tweet editor tries to make writing easy and thus include two buttons with the @ and # symbols, that allow you to create mentions and hashtags without needing to find the hidden buttons on your mobile. Click the # button and create a new hashtag by typing any word you want.

10. Now press the @ icon and see how the names of the users you follow are displayed.

11. Press the camera icon, select a photo from your library or take a new one, add the location, and, finally, click the **Tweet** button.

12. When you are back on your home page, slide a finger over one of the tweets on your timeline to display the options.

13. The first button allows you to respond to the tweet, the second retweets it, the third marks it as a favorite, and the fourth copies the URL or sends it by e-mail. If you are the author of the tweet, you can also erase it. Press the **Favorite** button of a tweet and see how it is displayed.

IMPORTANT

The application for iPhone allows you to access the **Connect** and **Discover** screens, which are almost identical to those on the website. The **Account** screen allows you to access your profile; send direct messages; access drafts, lists, and saved searches; and open the application's settings panel.

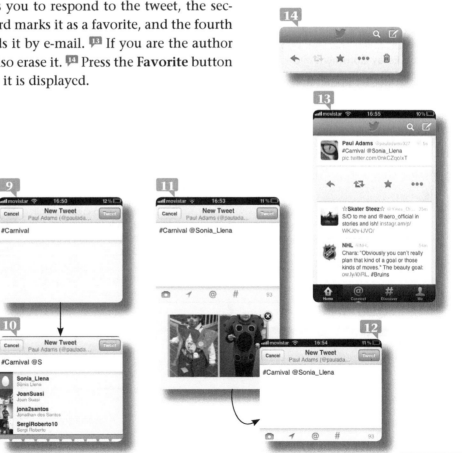

Publishing a poll on Twitter (I)

IMPORTANT

When you create a poll, in the **Type of Question** drop-down field, the **Multiple Choice** option creates a poll that allows various answers (select multiple answers) or only one (select only one answer). **Drop-down** creates a drop-down option field, **Matrix** creates a matrix, **Rating Scale** allows the evaluation of a group of elements, **Ranking** orders the elements presented by preference, **Single Textbox** creates a text box in simple text, **Twitter Comment** creates a 140-character box, and **Essay Comment** allows longer responses.

THE TWTPOLL WEBSITE ALLOWS YOU TO create a poll and publish it automatically in a tweet. You can access the service with your Twitter account, choose between different types of polls, and create your own questions and answers for your Twitter followers.

1. Go to **www.twtpoll.com**, but remain signed in to Twitter.
2. Click the **register / sign in** link in the header of the home page. 1
3. You do not need to create a new account. Click the **Sign in with Twitter** link to enter with your Twitter username. 2
4. Read the terms of service and, if you agree, click the **Authorize app** button so that Twtpoll can access your data on Twitter. 3
5. The header of the website indicates that you are logged into your Twitter account. Click the **Create a Poll** button. 4
6. The **Create Poll** page opens. The first expanding field, **Type of Question**, allows you to select the type of poll to be created. Open it.
7. Select the **Matrix** option, to create a grid in which different values are to be assigned to different options. 5
8. Write a question that you would like to ask your followers in the **Question** field.

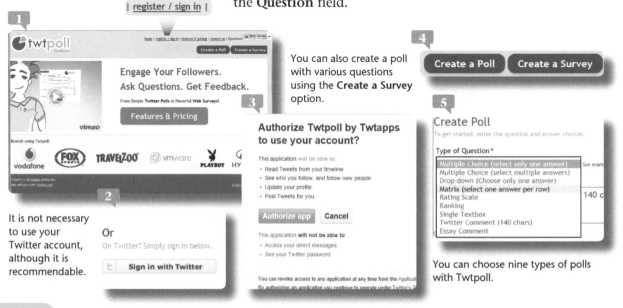

| register / sign in |

Engage Your Followers.
Ask Questions. Get Feedback.
From Simple **Twitter Polls** to Powerful **Web Surveys!**

Features & Pricing

vimeo

Brands using Twtpoll

vodafone FOX SPORTS TRAVELZOO vmware PLAYBOY HY

It is not necessary to use your Twitter account, although it is recommendable.

Or
On Twitter? Simply sign in below.

Sign in with Twitter

You can also create a poll with various questions using the **Create a Survey** option.

Authorize Twtpoll by Twtapps to use your account?

This application will be able to:
- Read Tweets from your timeline.
- See who you follow, and follow new people.
- Update your profile.
- Post Tweets for you.

Authorize app   Cancel

This application **will not be able to**:
- Access your direct messages.
- See your Twitter password

You can revoke access to any application at any time from the Applica
By authorizing an application you continue to operate under Twitter's T

Create a Poll   Create a Survey

Create Poll
To get started, enter the question and answer choices.

Type of Question *

Multiple Choice (select only one answer)
Multiple Choice (select multiple answers)
Drop-down (Choose only one answer)
Matrix (select one answer per row)
Rating Scale
Ranking
Single Textbox
Twitter Comment (140 chars)
Essay Comment

See exam

140 c

You can choose nine types of polls with Twtpoll.

9. In the **Column choices** you should type the different values that users could give to the options that will be shown. There should be one option per line.

10. In the **Row choices** field, you should type the options to be analyzed. As before, you should type one per line. When you have finished, click the **Continue** button. **6**

11. Expand the **End date** field to determine when the poll should be closed. You can choose a duration of anywhere between an hour to a month. Click the **Choose Date/Time** link.

12. You can give a precise date and time for concluding the poll. Click the date field to display the calendar and select a date. **7**

13. Use the following expandable fields to select an exact time and a time zone.

14. Expand the **Language** menu, choose the option you want and click **Continue**. **8**

15. Click the **Preview and Customize Your Poll** button to see how it looks **9** and then **Continue** followed by the **Activate Free Poll** button.

16. Modify the tweet that will contain the poll and click **Publish Now** to tweet it. **10**

6

Create Poll
To get started, enter the question and answer choices.

Type of Question *

Matrix (select one answer per row) ▾ See examples

Question *

Like singing...

Question about an Image / Video? ⑧

Column choices *

in the shower
while working
in my car
anywhere

Row choices *

I prefer dancing
Never
loudly

Continue
‹

7

Poll Details
Add more details about your poll.

End date *

03/05/2013 | 2 ▾ | : | 15 ▾ | am ▾ | GMT+0 Western Europe Time ▾

close

← March 2013 →

Su	Mo	Tu	We	Th	Fr	Sa
					1	2
3	4	5	6	7	8	9
10	11	12	13	14	15	16
17	18	19	20	21	22	23
24	25	26	27	28	29	30
31						

SEND AN EMAIL
TO THE FOUNDER

8

Language

English
French
German
Spanish
Portuguese
Italian
Other

tes per user

premium options?

questions, let us know: | SEND AN EMAIL
TO THE FOUNDER

9

Like singing...

	in the shower	while working	in my car	anywhere
I prefer dancing	○	○	○	○
Never	○	○	○	○
loudly	○	○	○	○

Vote See results

10

Publish this poll
Now that you have configured your poll, use the options below to publish and share it with your followers.

Twitter   Other Social Networks   Embed on your Website

Tweet now and setup automatic tweets throughout the week!
Schedule up to 10 tweet reminders for your followers to vote on your poll!

Tweet *
Change the tweet below to tweet NOW or SCHEDULE it.
You can also share it on other social networks or email. Simply use this link: **http://twtpoll.com/306iu2**

Do you like singing? #poll Like singing...
http://twtpoll.com/306iu2

72

Publish Now Schedule Tweet

SEND AN EMAIL

You can activate the **Allow multiple votes per user** option so that each user can vote more than once.

Publishing a poll on Twitter (II)

THE BEST THING ABOUT USING TWTPOLL to set up a poll that you would like to publish through Twitter is that it allows you to program up to ten different tweets that will be sent automatically just when you are ready.

1. Obtain a response to your poll and go to Twitter to see the tweet that was sent.

2. Click the **Expand** link to expand the field.

3. See that the poll has been conducted with Twtpoll by Twtapps. Click on the poll's link.

4. A Twtpoll page opens. In the right-hand corner the number of votes, the number of visits via the website, and the number of visits via mobile are displayed. Click the **Copy** button in the first section.

5. A new poll opens (identical to the original), which can be modified to create similar poll. Go back to the previous page.

6. The **Edit** button allows you to modify the poll until the moment when the first vote is registered. From that moment, you will only be allowed to change the closing date of the poll. Click the **See Results** button.

When you tweet a poll from Twtpoll, it is displayed as a link.

When a user goes to a poll, he or she will see it just as you do, but without the editing options.

7. The results are displayed as a bar graph. Now click the **Schedule Tweets** tab in the header. [4]

8. Twtpoll allows you to program up to ten tweets to be sent automatically when you wish. Modify the text of the next tweet you would like to send and, instead of clicking the **Publish Now** button, use the one called **Schedule Tweet**. [5]

9. Select a day, an hour, and a time zone, and then click the **Save** button. [6]

10. The programmed tweet is added to the list, but the word **Scheduled** is displayed in the **Sent** column to show that it has still to be sent.

11. You can send or program up to ten tweets. As they are sent, the respective **Schedule** buttons disappear and the page is updated. [7]

12. Click the **Other Social Networks** tab.

13. You can share the poll on Facebook, LinkedIn, Myspace Orkut, or by e-mail using the available buttons.

14. Now click the **Embed on your Website** tab. [8] This page generates an embedding code that allows you to publish your poll on any web page. You should decide whether to display the question, the results, or both, if it should appear in a sidebar or in a post, if it will have a transparent background, and, if you wish, the exact measurements.

IMPORTANT

Another online application that allows you to create polls is Pollowers. In this case both the question and the answers form a tweet, so that together they should occupy no more than 140 characters. Your followers should respond to the tweet, indicating their answers with a number that Pollowers will then process to obtain a result.

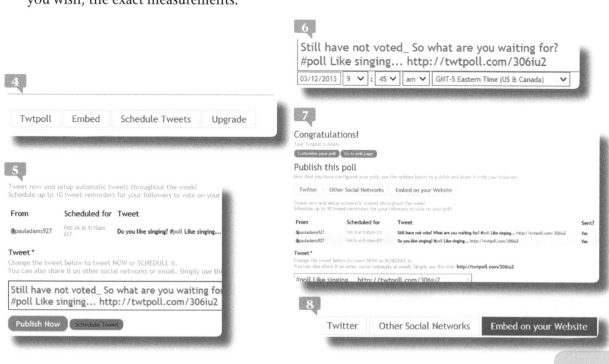

Displaying the last tweets on your blog

BOTH BLOGGER AND WORDPRESS.COM OFFER a widget that automatically displays your latest tweets. It is an easy way of offering snippets of information on your blog as well.

1. Choose a tweet that you would like to share in your blogs. Place the pointer over it and select **Expand** or **View photo**.

2. When the tweet expands, click the **Details** link. 📩

3. The tweet opens in a page that has a URL that does not expire: it is a permalink. You can copy the address from your address bar and share it by e-mail or another way. Click the **Embed Tweet** option. 📩

4. You can choose among an HTML code, a short code, or a link. Choose the type of code that you would like to generate, copy it 📩 and paste it where you would like it to be embedded. For example, this could be a post or a comment on a blog. Go to your blog's Dashboard on Blogger and click the **Layout** tab.

5. You are going to insert a gadget that displays your latest tweets. Click an **Add a Gadget link** 📩 that you like.

Details

You can permanently copy the URL of any tweet to share it on another platform or to use its embedding code for reproducing it in a post or a comment.

pic.twitter.com/onkCZqoIxT

6. In the panel on the left, click the **More Gadgets** tab 💬 and locate the **Twitter Updates 2.2: FeedWitter** gadget. 💬

7. Modify the title and introduce your **Twitter username** into the appropriate field (without the @ symbol). 💬

8. Make any additional changes, click the **Update** link in the preview, and click **Save**.

9. Click the **View Blog** link to check the result. 💬

10. Go to your WordPress.com blog and open the **Widgets** screen in the **Appearance** section.

11. Insert the **Twitter** widget 💬 into one of the sidebars.

12. Insert a name for the widget and your Twitter username.

13. You can configure it so that it does not display tweets from the Publicize tool, or retweets. You can also insert the **Follow Me** button and create a message that will be displayed in front of the time of publication. Make the changes you would like, click the **Save** button, 💬 and go to your blog to see how it differs from the Blogger widget. 💬

14. If you would like to show the latest tweets from different accounts, for example, from each of your authors, you can easily add a Twitter widget for each of them.

IMPORTANT

You can add a Follow on Twitter button by using the following code: [twitter-follow screen_name='USERNAME'] in the place you would like to embed it. If you would prefer that your username is not displayed next to the word Follow, add the following text in front of the square bracket: show_screen_name='no'. To add the number of followers, add the text: show_count='yes'.

In the next exercise you will learn how to create a customized widget.

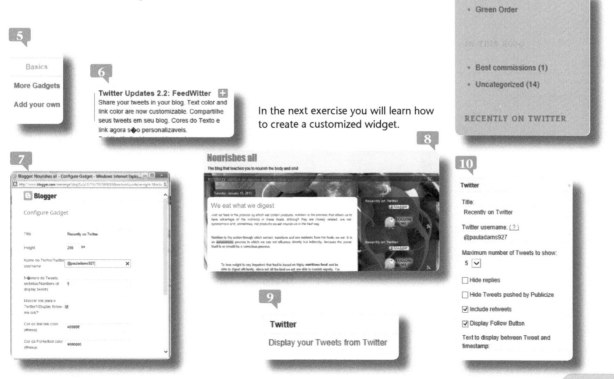

Creating your own Twitter widget

TWITTER ALLOWS YOU TO CREATE YOUR own widget, with customized colors, that shows much more than your latest tweets. It does this instantly. When you have finished designing the widget, it gives you an HTML code that you can embed into a widget on your blog.

1. Go to the web page **https://twitter.com/about/resources/widgets**.

2. On the next page, click on the **Create new** button. **1**

3. You can create different, interesting widgets. Click **Search**. **2**

4. An options' page and a sample widget for a specific search are displayed. To the right there is a preview of the widget that displays the most recent tweets related to the search in real time. In the **Search Query** field, type a new search word, something relevant to you, preceded by a hashtag (#). **3**

5. Click the **Preview** section to see the results. **4**

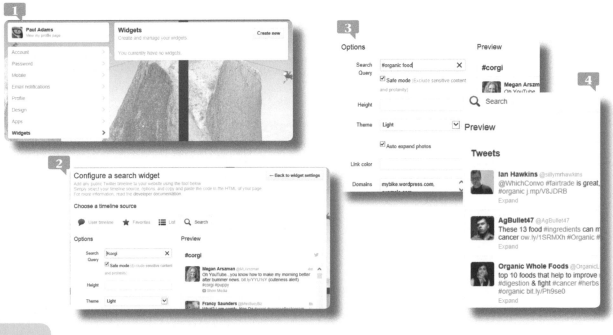

6. From the **Options** section you can change some things about the appearance, like height and theme. Choose the **Dark** option on the **Theme** menu. **5** The result is updated instantly. **6**

7. Make any other modifications to the color if you want and click the **Create widget** button. **7**

8. You can now copy the link into the HTML text of a post in your WordPress.com or Blogger blog. To do that, right-click the code and choose **Copy**. **8**

9. Go to your Blogger blog and find the HTML code of a post, for example. There, paste the code from the widget that you have created. **9**

10. Update the post and preview it. **10**

11. If the widget is not placed correctly in the post, go back to the previous page and copy the code in another point.

IMPORTANT

You can also create a widget that plays your last tweets, your favorite tweets (giving you much more control over the content displayed, but less variety), or the tweets from your lists (this will allow you to share your clients' tweets, for example).

Creating a Facebook account

FACEBOOK IS CURRENTLY THE ULTIMATE SOCIAL network. With 845 million users, it is an indispensable communication tool for small businesses. As you know, you must be a part of it.

1. Create a Facebook account if you do not already have one. Go to the website **www.facebook.com**, fill in the form, and click **Sign Up.** 📝

2. The first thing to do when you enter Facebook is to make friends (which is what a social network is for). To this end, the service offers to search your e-mail account. If you wish to do so, click the **Find Friends** button, 📝 and after signing up to Google allow Facebook to access your account data. 📝

3. Should you wish to import data from **Gmail**, you will need to export the data beforehand. Go to your e-mail account and, as explained on the Facebook web page that you now have open on your screen, export the contact that you would like to find on Facebook. To do so, go to your contacts page, select those who you would like to locate, and select the **Export** option form the **More** menu. 📝 Keep the **Google CSV format (for importing into a Google Account)** format selected in the dialog box that opens, click the **Export** button 📝 and save the file.

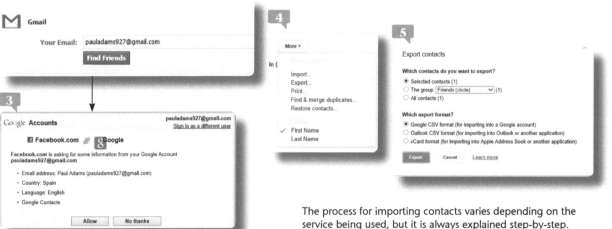

The process for importing contacts varies depending on the service being used, but it is always explained step-by-step.

4. Go back to the Facebook page that you left open, click the **Open Folder** button and locate the exported file.

5. The contacts that coincide with the data given soon appear. Keep the ones that you wish to import selected and click the **Add to Friends** button.

6. An invitation has been sent to those who have a Facebook profile and you are now given the option to invite the rest to form part of your community.

7. When you have checked your e-mail accounts, skip the step for the next search and complete the profile information. **6**

8. As you type in the various fields, suggestions will help you complete the information faster. When you finish, click the **Save & Continue** button. **7**

9. Choose a photo for your profile and save the changes. **8**

10. In the **Search** field, introduce the name of a friend you would like to add. Pages, applications, and people that match the search data are displayed. **9** If none coincide, click the **See more results for** link.

11. When you click **Add Friend** **10** a friend request will be sent that the invitee will have to accept to be included in your network.

IMPORTANT

If you click the Friends link in your biography, you will go to a page where all of your friends are displayed. Here the **+1 Add Friend** button leads to another where you can find new friends using filters such as Hometown, Current Location, College or University, Secondary School, etc.

Later, you can add much more information to your profile and decide what you would like to share and what you would not.

When you have completed the signing up process, you will be able to find friends, one by one, by their name or by their e-mail.

Setting up your profile and beginning to interact

YOUR FACEBOOK PROFILE CAN INCLUDE A great deal of information. In this exercise you will begin to add information and interact with your friends on Facebook.

1. Go to your timeline by clicking on your image in the header of the page **1** and click the **Update Info** button. **2**

2. Complete all the information that you consider relevant, organized in different modules. **3** You should be extremely careful about what you publish on your profile, as it will define what we call today the **online reputation**. When you have finished editing each module, click **Save**. **4**

3. Next to many fields is an icon that indicates the presence of a drop-down menu. Click on them to choose if the information given is to be public, private, shared exclusively with friends, or reserved for specific groups. **5**

4. When you have finished, go back to your timeline.

5. Whenever you receive a friend request, the **Friends** icon lights up on the right of the application's header. Use the drop-down menu in question and either accept or click the **Not**

1

2

Welcome to Your Profile
This is your place to collect photos, interests, and life events that tell your story on Facebook.

Start Tour

Add a Cover

Paul Adams Update Info Activity Log

Update Info

3

Paul Adams About

Work and Education Done Editing

Where have you worked?

San Francisco Chronicle
Publisher/Editor

• Add a Project

Where did you go to college?

University of San Francisco

• Add a Class

Where did you go to high school?

History by Year

1974
Born on February 1, 1974

About You Edit

Write About Yourself

Basic Info

Birthday February 1, 1974

Sex Male

4

Save Cancel

5

Where did you go to high school?

Los Angeles High School Edit

• Add a Class

✓ 🌐 Public
👥 Friends
🔒 Only Me
⚙ Custom

☆ Close Friends
👪 Family
See all lists...

Living

San Francisco, California
Current City

6

Friend Requests Find Friends · Settings

Sônia Llena Hurtado Confirm Not Now

People You May Know

If you select the Not Now option, you can accept the friend request later. The user will not receive a notification.

Now button. When you do this, proposals for new friends who have been selected for their profile and their accepted and invited friends appear at the bottom of the menu.

6. The next icon, **Messages**, allows you to write new messages or to access existing ones. Open it and click the **Send a New Message** link.

7. As you begin to type in the name field, coinciding options are displayed. Remember that messages sent using this function are private. Send one.

8. The third menu in this block, **Notifications**, informs you about all sorts of activities in your network: whenever a friend writes in his or her biography, accepts a friend request, or comments on one of your photographs, to give a few examples. If you click on the notification, you will be sent to the content it refers to.

9. When a user comments on your timeline, they have various options. You can express that you **Like** it with a click or comment on a friend's publication. You can also **Unfollow** the post and see your friend's details. The friend will receive a notification for both actions.

IMPORTANT

Facebook will use the information given to try to relate it to other people. Thus, in the bar on the right of the home page, names of people you might know are proposed.

Setting up your account and your information

IMPORTANT

Remember that if you make your personal information public, it can be used by anyone as they wish. Since you can decide what you share with whom, keep your personal information for friends and make public only the more general information.

WHEN YOU CREATE A USERNAME IN FACEBOOK, it is important to set up the account and privacy settings according to how you will use it. Obviously, your requirements will be different if you want to create a professional profile rather than simply to contact friends.

1. Click the cog button to the right of the **Home** button and select the **Account Settings** option. 1

2. On the **General Account Settings** page that opens by default, you can establish some main settings. 2 Click the **Edit** button in the Networks panel. 3

3. Click the **Join a Network** link and, in the **Network name** field, type the name of your city.

4. Various related networks are displayed. 4 Select one of them and save the changes or click the **Cancel** button.

5. Examine the other sections that you might wish to edit, click the **Security** tab 5 and check all the security settings that Facebook offers. For the moment we recommend that you activate **Secure Browsing**. 6

6. Activate the **Notifications** tab to determine which actions you would like to be notified about by e-mail. Click the **Edit**

Create an Ad
Account Settings
Privacy Settings
Log Out

Help

General Account Settings

Name	Paul Adams
Username	You have not set a username.
Email	Primary: pauladams927@gmail.com
Password	Password never changed.
Networks	No networks.
Language	English (US)

Download a copy of your Facebook data.

English (US)

data.

3

✎ Edit

Each of the categories can hide many options.

5

⚙ General
🛡 Security

Network name: San Francisco

San Francisco Art Inst.
San Francisco, Califor...
University of San Fra...
San Francisco, Califor...
S.F. State
San Francisco, Califor...
Academy of Art
San Francisco, Califor...
Lowell High
San Francisco, Califor...

Save Changes | Cancel

6

Security Question	Setting a security question will help us identify you.
Secure Browsing	☑ Browse Facebook on a secure connection (https) when possible
	Save Changes	Cancel
Login Notifications	Login notifications are disabled.

4

7

🔲 On Facebook | All notifications, sounds on | View
✉ Email | You'll receive:
    ⦿ All notifications, except the ones you unsubscribe from
    ○ Only notifications about your account, security and privacy
    Close
🔔 Push notifications | Some notifications | View
📱 Text message | Text notifications are turned off | Edit
👤 Activity that involves | On | View

button in each field, select those actions you would like to be notified about, and save the changes.

7. Click the **Followers** tab, read the explanation and turn it on as it is deactivated by default.

8. A **Follow** button will appear in your profile. It is accessible to all Facebook users unless it has been blocked. All of your public updates will be received by your followers as well as your friends although your followers can also select the type of notifications that they would like to receive.

9. A series of options are added. Click on the **Edit** link of the Twitter section and click the **Link profile to Twitter** button.

10. Sign in and allow the application to access your account.

11. You are informed that all public actions on Facebook will be published automatically on Twitter. Click **Save Changes**.

12. Open the drop-down menu in the top right-hand corner and select the **Privacy Settings** option.

13. Read the information offered and the various categories proposed, and define a predetermined privacy setting for each of them.

IMPORTANT

The **Ads** page in **Account Settings** allows you to determine the type of actions related to advertisers that can be shared with your Facebook friends.

Ads

Always be careful with your privacy settings.

Updating your timeline

YOUR FACEBOOK TIMELINE IS BUILT, among other things, from your status updates that allow you to explain what you are doing at each moment, with whom and where, to whomever you want.

1. In your timeline, below the header panel, you will find the **Status** panel. Type text that you would like to share with your friends in it.

2. Click the first button below the Status Bar that displays an avatar icon with a + sign.

3. You can explain who you are with at this moment. When you start to type a name in the expanded field, coinciding options are displayed and you can select any of them with a click. Click the next button (the clock icon).

4. You can also share past events and include them in your timeline, indicating the exact moment in which they occurred. Try it now.

5. Click the next button and add a location.

When you begin to write a name, names of friends that coincide are displayed.

When you add past events, you complete your timeline.

6. Click the fourth button and note that you can change the privacy setting for this particular post. **5** Click the **Post** button.

7. If you have assigned a past date, the status update enters the timeline at the indicated date. You can access it with the timeline browser in the upper right-hand corner. **6** Place it and click the **Share** button. **7**

8. Open the **Share** menu: You can post it on your own timeline (which has already been done), on that of a friend, in a group, or in a private message to a friend so that only they can see it. Select the second option. **8**

9. In the first field, write the name of a Facebook friend and in the second, a message that can be seen by anyone who accesses the two timelines. When you have finished, click the **Share Status** link. **9**

10. Go to your friend's wall and see the result. Note that you can also like it, comment on it, or share it again. **10**

11. Go back to the post that you created in Facebook, place the pointer over it, click the button with a pencil icon, and check your editing options. **11**

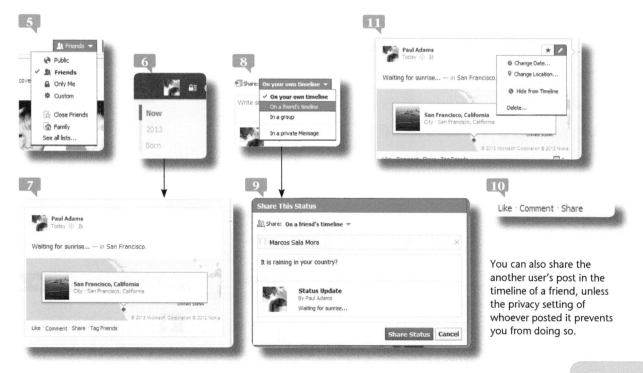

You can also share the another user's post in the timeline of a friend, unless the privacy setting of whoever posted it prevents you from doing so.

Publishing photos and videos

YOU CAN INSERT BOTH PHOTOS AND videos into your status updates or your private messages, create albums, tag people who appear in them and assign a location to each photo.

1. Click the **Photo** tab in the status update box in your timeline.

2. Click the **Upload Photos/Video** tab 🔳 and select a video file for this exercise.

3. The process for uploading a photo is almost identical. Configure other aspects of the status update as you please, just as you did in the previous exercise. Click the **Post** button. 🔳

4. Wait for the video to upload. Then click **Edit Video**. 🔳

5. Complete the form that appears and click the **Save** button. 🔳

6. You might have to wait for the video to be codified. When the process has finished you will receive a notification. 🔳 Click on it.

You can upload a photo or a video to share with whoever you wish, take a photo instantly with your webcam, or create a photo album.

Facebook accepts almost any type of video file, although MP4 is the format that works best, and the aspect ratio should be between 9 x 16 and 16 x 9.

7. The video appears just as it will be seen by your friends. At the bottom of the screen there are options that allow you to modify any aspect of its configuration. Click on the **Edit This Video** link. 6

8. Click the arrowhead buttons below the frame sample and choose one of the suggested images. 7 When you have finished click **Save** and check the result in your timeline and then on your home page.

9. Click the photos section on your timeline 8 to access your photos and videos. Then click the **Add Photos** button and choose some images from your computer.

10. The images begin to load into an album. As they are processed, you can insert captions, 9 change the order of the images, or indicate the location of each one. The faces are automatically framed. 10 Click on one of them.

11. A field opens in which you can say who it is. If you type the name of a Facebook friend, the photo is associated with his or her profile. 11

12. Type a name for the album, a description, and a location in the header.

13. The buttons at the bottom of the window allow you to add more photos, upload them with a high resolution, change the privacy, or post them. Post them.

You can edit the video's information and choose the icon that will identify it.

Converting your profile into a public page

FACEBOOK ALSO ALLOWS YOU TO CREATE a web page (ideal for businesses) as it offers more suitable features. Furthermore, you should take into account that, just as with profiles of individuals, Facebook can eliminate it if it does not follow the rules set forth in its policy. If you start with a personal page and your business takes off, the good news is that you can transfer your profile to a web page.

1. To create a web page in Facebook you must go to the bottom of any page in the social network and click the **Create a Page** link.

2. However, you can also convert your personal profile into a public web page. Go to your account's settings page, click the **Download a copy of your Facebook data** link, and follow the instructions to carry out the download. This could take a few hours.

3. When you have completed the download, go to the **https://www.facebook.com/pages/create.php?migrate** web page.

4. Once there, select the most suitable business type, choose a category, complete the requested information, and click the **Get Started** button. Its name should be the same as or similar to that of your profile.

1

About   Create an Ad   Create a Page

2

General Account Settings

Name	Paul Adams
Username	You have not set a username.
Email	Primary: pauladams927@gmail.com
Password	Password never changed.
Networks	No networks.
Language	English (US)

Download a copy of your Facebook data.

Download a copy of your Facebook data.

It is very important that you select the appropriate business type and category for your business.

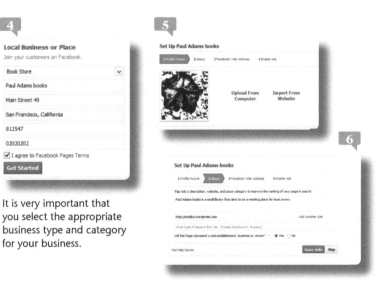

5. Accept the warning, take into account the fact that you will not be able to recuperate your profile information, and click the **Migrate** button.

6. You can keep your profile photo or upload a new one. Modify it and click the **Next** button or click the **Skip** button.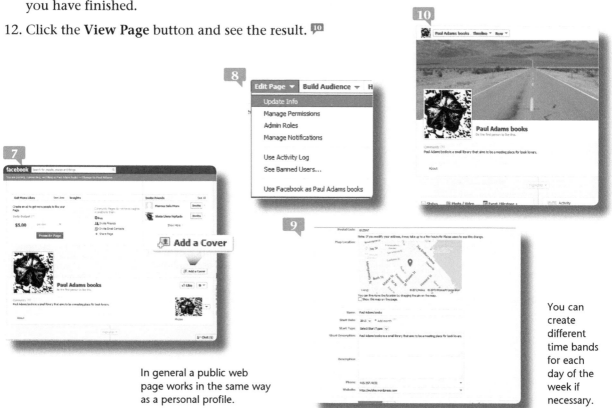

7. Complete the information that you are asked for, including your Twitter URL, and click the **Save Info** button.

8. You have created your web page. Those who were once your friends are now followers of those who like your page. Unzip the export file of your profile.

9. Click **Add Cover** and, just as you did for your profile, load your previous cover photo. You will find it in the **Photos/Cover Photos** folder of the exported file.

10. In the header of the Admin panel, expand the **Edit Page** menu and select the **Update Info** option.

11. Modify the data if you wish. Remember that you can open the files of the HTML folder that you downloaded from your previous profile and copy data from it. Save the changes when you have finished.

12. Click the **View Page** button and see the result.

IMPORTANT

In the **Edit Page** menu you can select the **Manage Permissions** option. This takes you to some settings parameters where you can make your page not visible while you finish editing it, restrict its visibility by country or by age, establish who can post, enable the **Messages** button, and ban certain offensive terms. Configure it to suit your needs.

In general a public web page works in the same way as a personal profile.

You can create different time bands for each day of the week if necessary.

Managing a page with various administrators

IMPORTANT

To get the most out of your page, you should interact intensely with other users, not only through Facebook, but also via other media (your Twitter account and your blog for example). Encourage your followers to click the **Like** and **Follow** buttons. Publish on all platforms often and link them to save time and effort.

YOUR FACEBOOK PAGE CAN ALSO BE managed by various administrators simultaneously, or allow partial permissions for certain actions. The administrators can post in the name of the page or personally, using their own username.

1. On your Facebook page, expand the **Edit Page** menu and select the **Admin Roles** option.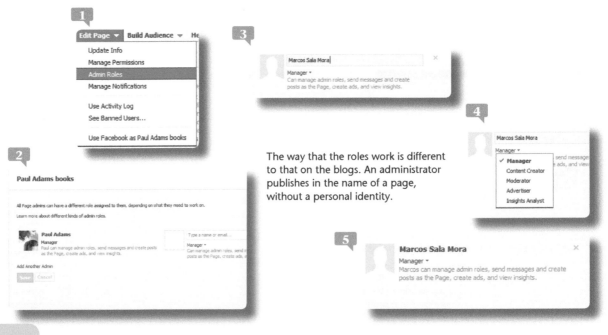

2. From this page, you can authorize other users to access your Facebook page with certain privileges. In the **Type a name or e-mail** field type the e-mail address of a Facebook follower whom you would like to authorize (take into account that you cannot invite a user who does not follow you).

3. Open the following menu that now shows the **Manager** option.

4. A **Manager** has absolute permissions, but can give restricted permissions: an **Insights Analyst** has the most limited permissions as he or she can only consult the statistics. The **Advertiser** can create publicity ads as well, and the **Moderator** can also manage comments and send messages in the page's name. Finally, a **Content Creator** (in addition to all

The way that the roles work is different to that on the blogs. An administrator publishes in the name of a page, without a personal identity.

the above) can also create content in the name of the page, edit it, and add applications. Keep the **Manager** option for this exercise 🔲 and click the **Save** button.

5. Enter your password to confirm the invitation and see how the invited user is immediately added. 🔲

6. The second administrator will receive a notification of the invitation 🔲 and, on clicking it, will access the page where he or she can check what types of rights have been granted. The second administrator can begin a tour of the various options on the page. 🔲

7. An administrator can begin to edit or to create a status update at any moment. Any update will be published in the name of the page without revealing the person's identity. 🔲

8. The **Identity** option in the header allows the administrator to reveal his or her identity without having to leave the page. On changing to a personal identity, 🔲 the administrator can share content at a personal level. 🔲 In this case they are considered to be publications and not status updates. The Manager will receive a notification of the personal post, but not of the status updates. On clicking on one of these notifications, the post will open alone on a page. 🔲

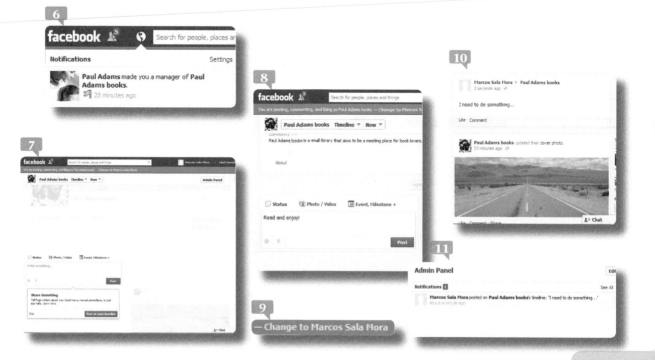

Creating an ad

FACEBOOK ALLOWS YOU TO CREATE AN ad or a sponsored story that has a spectacular following extremely easily. In this exercise you will simulate creating one and will get a real estimate.

1. You can create an ad, define it to the last detail, find out the daily fee, and preview it free of charge, although you will need to have paid previously to publish it. At the bottom of your page, click the **Create an Ad** link. 🔲

2. On the next page, where you can find some information about creating an ad on Facebook, click the **Create an Ad** button. 🔲

3. In the first field that opens, you must establish to which page you wish users to be sent when they click on the ad. Type the address of your blog (Blogger or Wordpress.com) in the **Choose a Facebook destination or enter a URL** field. 🔲

4. The page is updated to help you customize the advertisement. In the **Your Ad** section, type a headline and the text for your ad.

5. Click the **Update Image** button and select one of the photos in it for the ad. 🔲

6. In the **Right Column Preview** panel you already have a preview of your ad. 🔲 Go to the **Choose Your Audience** module.

IMPORTANT

As you introduce data about your audience, the **Audience** section is updated and displays the approximate number of users to whom your ad could be shown.

Audience

973,180 people
- who live in the United States
- who live within 10 miles of San Francisco, CA

1

About   Create an Ad   Create a Page   Deve

Facebook © 2013 · English (US)

2

🔍 Search for people, places and things

⊙ **Advertise on Facebook**

Over 1 billion people. We'll help you reach the right ones.

Create an Ad

verview

It Works

Stories

Step 1: Build your Facebook Page

Step 2: Connect with people

Step 3: Engage your audience

3

Choose a Facebook destination or enter a URL: http://mybyke.wordpress.com/

🔒 Suggest an ad

4

Your Ad

Headline: [?]   16 characters left
My bike

Text: [?]   35 characters left
This is a page of a lover of cycling and healthy living

Image: [?]   ← 100 px →
Upload Image
or Choose From Image Library   72 px

Related Page: [?]
☐ Show social activity about mybike next to my ad

Right Column Preview

My bike

This is a page of a lover of cycling and healthy living

The ad text cannot have more than 90 characters (50 less than a tweet!) so you should be clear and concise.

7. You should now define the criteria. Eliminate the predetermined country by clicking on its cross icon and indicate the countries that you would like to reach.

8. You can further define the reach of the ad to a city or a province. Do so if you wish to.

9. Set the age group and gender for your audience. 6

10. The **Precise Interests** section is more interesting. Click on one of the categories to see its subcategories and select the ones you want. Note that you can select subcategories for various categories. For each of them, the number of chosen selections is indicated. 7

11. In the **Campaign, Pricing and Schedule** module, you can obtain a detailed estimate. Define the currency and the payment country.

12. Expand the second part of the **Campaign Budget** section field and choose the **Lifetime Budget** option. 8

13. Select a start time and an end time for the campaign and note how the budget changes.

14. In the **Pricing** section you can decide if you prefer to pay per click (CPC) or per showing. In the latter case, the cost is less. Click the **Review Ad** button, check the details, 9 and click the Facebook logo to go back to your page.

IMPORTANT

The final price for your ad will depend on the number of advertisers that are competing for the same audience; the greater the competition, the higher the price. However, you will never pay more than your bid or your total budget.

195

Managing photos on your page

THE MANAGEMENT OF PHOTOS ON A web page is no different than doing so on a private profile. You will see that in this exercise and will also get to know the albums' editing options.

1. In your computer's browser, decompress and open the file of your previous personal profile that you had downloaded.

2. Open the **HTML** folder ![1] and double-click on the **Wall** file to open your old profile's wall. ![2] Click on any link to access the contents. ![3]

3. Go back to the folder, check that all the images that were contained in the profile's **Photos** folder are there, and load them into a new album. The process is the same as that described for the personal profiles.

4. When you have finished, click on the **Photos** section in your Facebook page and open the album that has been created. ![4]

5. Click the **Edit** link. ![5]

6. You can now insert comments on the photos or edit them (if you have not already done so). Try it.

If you would like to recycle text from your old profile, you will have to copy it and past it into your page.

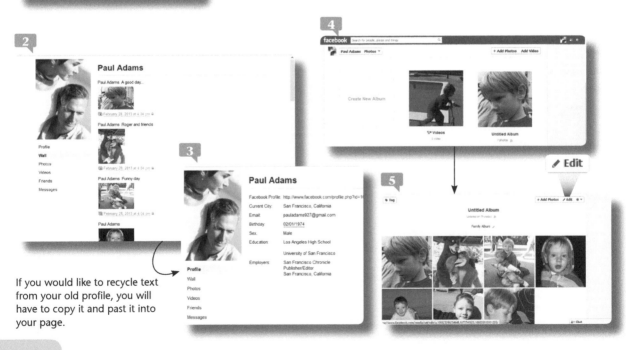

7. Place the pointer over one of the photos and, when the arrow-head icon appears, click on it to display the options.

8. You can move the photo to another album, set it as the album cover, or eliminate it. Click the second option and click the **Done** button in the header.

9. You can also reorganize your photos on the screen that displays your photos in your album without needing to enter the editing mode. Click on one of the photos to display its page.

10. Place the pointer over the photo to display the options, click on **Options** and select **Rotate Left**.

11. The image rotates. Rotate it to the right if necessary and click the **Share** option.

12. You can share the photo on your own timeline, on a friend's timeline, in a group, or on your page. Choose the option you want, type a message and click the **Share Photo** button.

13. Click the **Edit** button in the panel on the right.

14. Once again you have the opportunity to modify the comment, the people tagged, and the date. Click the button that displays the privacy options to open its options menu. Select the one called **Edit Album Privacy**.

15. In the **Edit Album** box, you can modify the name, the description, and the location. You cannot modify the privacy of an album in a web page because a web page is, by definition, public. Click **Save** to finish.

IMPORTANT

To publish your blog's posts, click the **Sharing** option in the **Settings** tab on your WordPress.com Dashboard. In the **Publicize** section, click the **Add New Facebook Connection** link, set the level of privacy, click **Go to Post**, select what you would like to share, and click the **Allow** button. If you wish, create links to the other social networks that you use.

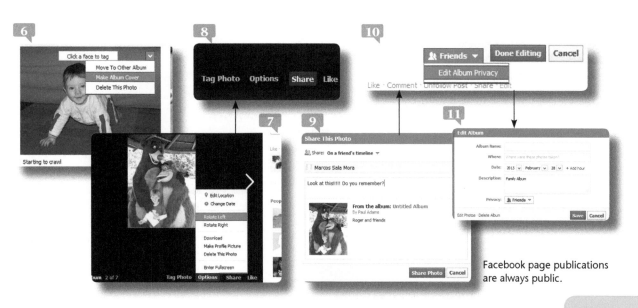

Facebook page publications are always public.

Promoting an event through Facebook

FACEBOOK'S EVENTS APPLICATION is an ideal way to promote that special event you are preparing. It allows you to define the event, interact with the guests, share files, and estimate the attendance.

1. For this exercise, you will imagine that your business is organizing an event that you would like to publicize through Facebook. In the **Favorites** section of the main page of Facebook, click on the **Events** section ▣ and click on the **Create Event** button. ▣

2. A form appears in which you should fill in the details of the event. Do so and, when you have finished, click **Create**. ▣

3. A page is created for the programmed event. Click the **Add Event Photo** button, ▣ upload an image and save changes.

4. Networks exist to generate interaction. Click on the **Ask Question** link. ▣

5. Type a question in the field that opens and click the **Add Poll Options** link. ▣

1

Paul Adams

FAVORITES
- Welcome
- News Feed
- Messages
- Events
- Photos
- Find Friends

2

+ Create Event | Today

3

Create New Event

Name	Divergent Bicycle meeting
Details	A space in which we find those who have some special bikes
Where	Main Street, U.S.A.
When	3/22/2013 10:30 pm PST End time?
Privacy	Friends of Guests

Invite Friends | Create | Cancel

4

Add Event Photo

Invite Friends | Edit

5

Divergent Bicycle meeting

6

Write Post | Add Photo / Video | Ask Question

Would you like to join us?

Add Poll Options | Divergent Bicycle meeting | Post

7

Would you like to join us?

+ Yes
+ Sorry, I can't
+ Maybe
+ Add an option...

☑ Allow anyone to add options | Divergent Bicycle meeting | Post

When you create a question, you can accept open answers.

6. You can add as many answer options as you like by typing them next to the **Plus (+)** signs. When you have finished, click **Post**.

7. Open the **Options** menu, select the **Edit Hosts** option and, in the box with the same name, type the names of the people who will be hosting the event.

8. Just as you are advised, before they can be shown as hosts, they must join the event. Click the **Submit** button.

9. You can still change the information about the event or edit it, add photos, links, or other posts. Click the **Share** link at the **Going** section of the event.

10. Create text that will advertise the event and click the **Share Event** button.

11. People who follow your page will receive a notification about the post and will be able to see it on your home page. A link called **Join** invites them to participate.

12. The name of those taking part and the total number of confirmed attendees are shown in the panel on the left. Click the **Export** link.

13. In the **Export Event** box, choose the **Send to e-mail** option with your e-mail address and click the **Export** button.

14. You will receive an .ics file by e-mail. When you open it, it automatically adds the event to your calendar.

The organizers should confirm that they will attend the event beforehand, or join it (which is the same).

Managing your Face-book page from iPhone

IMPORTANT

Facebook applications for mobiles are ideal for efficient and continuous management of your page, as it allows you to be connected with your community at all times and offer an immediate response to its concerns. Although you can manage your page from the Facebook for mobiles application, **Facebook's Pages Manager** is easier to use.

THERE IS AN APPLICATION SPECIFICALLY CREATED for managing your Facebook pages. It is currently available for iOS only.

1. For this exercise you will work from your mobile. Before starting, download the **Facebook Pages Manager** application.

2. Open the application, log in to Facebook and allow it to access your Facebook account. When you have completed the process, you will see your page on the screen.

3. In the header bar, click the Facebook friends icon. If there is a number on the right, this represents the number of new followers that the page has.

4. A list of all users who have **Liked** the page is displayed, and the names of the new followers are shown on a yellow background to highlight.

5. If you click on one of them you will access their profile, if it is not private.

6. Exactly the same as on you web page, the second icon in the header allows you to access your messages, and the third (the planet earth icon) opens the most recent notifications. Expand it to try it out. **6**

7. Close the panel again and now click the **Share Photo** tab.

8. You can now create a new photo or select one from the library. Choose the first option, take the photo and click the **Use** button.

9. Insert a comment for the photo, choose which album in which you would like to place it, and click the **Post** button. **7**

10. The page updates instantly. If you would like to introduce a status update, do so using the **Update Status** tab.

11. When the process has finished, click the **Filter** button.

12. You can use the filter to show your posts only, those of other people, or just the hidden ones. **8** Select **Others' Posts**.

13. Now click the **Comment** button for any of the filtered posts on the screen and type a reply comment for it. **9**

14. Click the **Comment** button to finish your post and then click the **Like** button.

15. To return to the general view of the page, click the button with the arrow pointing to the left. **10**

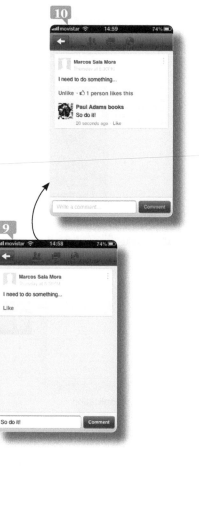

Accessing the stats

IF YOUR FACEBOOK PAGE IS USED for business, it is very important to be constantly aware of its statistics. You can take advantage of them when you have more than thirty followers.

1. Click the button on the top left-hand corner of the **Facebook Pages Manager** application to access its menu and click the **Insights** option. ▣

2. On this page, the total number of users that have clicked the **Like** button are displayed as well as the number of people that are **Talking About This** (those who have produced a story by commenting on, posting, or liking it), and the **Weekly Total Reach**. This last figure refers to the number of people who have seen content that is related to the page. ▣ At the bottom you will find a Trends chart that displays these last values. ▣

3. When your page has thirty followers, open it on your computer and, click the **See All** link in the statistics chart. ▣

4. In the upper part of this window the general statistics are displayed again. Place the pointer on any part of the chart to see its value as a tag. ▣

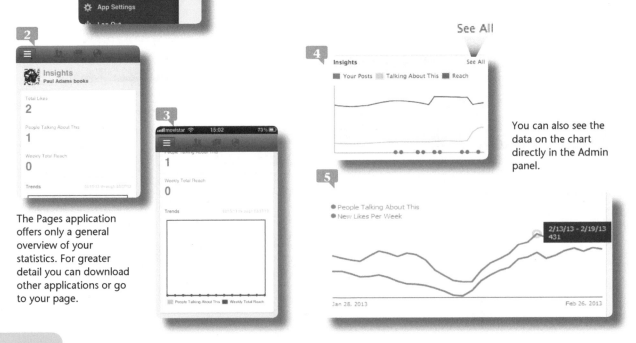

The Pages application offers only a general overview of your statistics. For greater detail you can download other applications or go to your page.

You can also see the data on the chart directly in the Admin panel.

5. Each of your posts is analyzed at the bottom. Place the pointer on the question mark to the right of each of the column headlines to see a description of its content.

6. Click on any of the column headlines.

7. The data are reorganized depending on the values. Now click the Reach value of any post.

8. Displayed graphically is the number of people who have seen the content directly on your page (organic), via ads (paid), or via an action of one of your friends (viral).

9. Click on the values of the columns called **Users That Interact** and **People Talking About This** and observe the charts.

10. In the upper part of the page, click the **Like** link and observe the stratification of data by gender, age, origin, and language that is offered, as well as the chart at the bottom.

11. Click **See Likes** to access a list of all the people who have liked your page and then close the box.

12. Now click the **Reach** tab in the header and check all the data in this section about the people who have seen posts related to your page.

13. To conclude, check the data of the people who are talking about your page by clicking the last tab.

IMPORTANT

The **Export** option on the different insights pages allow you to export the data to an Excel document.

The reach represents your page's potential followers. Study its demographic profile and create strategies to attract them.

Day to day with Instagram photos

INSTAGRAM IS MADE FOR CREATING, EDITING, applying filters, and sharing photos on social networks. It has a simple editor that offers really great results and allows you to distribute content on various networks.

1. Download the Instagram application on your mobile 🗨 and register by inserting the data requested. 🗨

2. Instagram allows you to find friends on your mobile 🗨 and on your Facebook account. Of the available methods offered, use one to start setting up a network. When you have finished click the **Next** button.

3. Instagram suggests some users to follow. Make any selections you want and click on **Done**.

4. Click the button in the center of the bottom of the screen to activate the camera and take a photo using the center button. 🗨

5. The available filters appear under the photo. 🗨 Try them one by one and choose one for your first Instagram photograph. 🗨

6. Click the second button over the filters.

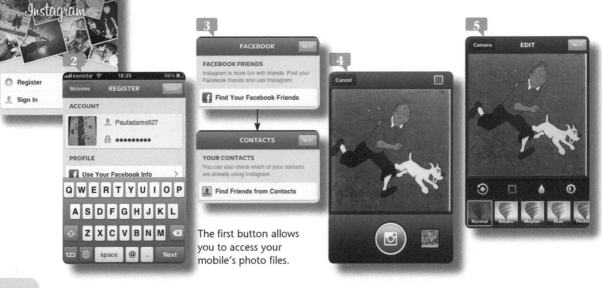

The first button allows you to access your mobile's photo files.

7. By doing this you have applied a toothed frame. The first button in the header rotates the photo, the third activates the **Tilt** effects, and the fourth applies more brightness. Click the third one and note how the greater part of the image becomes covered with something that looks like mist.

8. Drag your finger over the screen. The part of the image that you would like to highlight becomes clear.

9. When you move your finger away, a light blur is applied to the entire image except for the area that was clear. To erase the effect use the drop-down menu again and press the cross icon. If you press the circular icon, the effect is applied to a circular area.

10. Press the **Next** button to save the photo.

11. The **Share Photo** screen is displayed. You can now share the photo directly via Facebook, Twitter, e-mail, Tumblr, Flickr, or Foursquare. Select the **Facebook** option, allow the application to use your data and set whether or not you would like to share the Instagram photos that you like on Facebook.

12. Now select the Twitter option and introduce your data for this application and for any other account that you might wish to use.

13. Type a description for the image, press the **Share** button, and go to the next exercise.

IMPORTANT

Once you have linked your Instagram account to your Facebook account, a shortcut to Instagram appears on your Facebook menu. The same occurs when you link to Foursquare or any other application.

The button in the upper left-hand corner closes the camera.

By dragging two fingers across the screen, you can modify the size of the blurred area and its width.

Setting up your Instagram account and profile

YOU CAN ALSO SEARCH FOR USERS and photos on Instagram by using keywords. If you access your Settings options, you will also be able to define a public as well as a private profile.

1. When you share a photo, it is displayed on screen just as other users see it. Press the second button at the bottom of the screen.

2. You can begin to explore other users' photos by browsing the thumbnails or by using the search field to locate a user or a theme. Enter a word that is related to something that interests you, press the **Tags** tab (you can also search for users who use this word in their name) and then click on the **Search** button.

3. The number of photos available for the search word is indicated with all of its variations. Select one, see the photos that are displayed, and press on one of them to enlarge it.

4. Go to the bottom part of the screen and press the **Like** button.

5. Press the last button on the screen's bottom bar.

6. Your Instagram profile is displayed, where the number of published photos, your followers, and the people who are

If you carry out searches with keywords you will find interesting images to share with your followers on Instagram and other networks.

following you are displayed, among other things. Press on the **Edit Your Profile** text.

7. Complete the details of your public profile, complete your private profile, which only your friends can access, and click on **Save**.

8. Press **Settings** in the top right-hand corner of the screen.

9. From this screen you can find and invite your contacts from other applications to follow you. You can also do so using their e-mail addresses. You can access the photos you like on Instagram, close the session, configure the service, clear the search history, or mark all of your photos as private. Furthermore, in this last section, you can decide if you want to save photos with filters in your album. By default, only photos with a filter are saved. Click the **Share Settings** option.

10. From the screen that opens you can configure any of the services on the list, unlink accounts, or create new authorizations. Make the changes that you would like and return to the Options page.

11. Take into account that those accounts whose icons are displayed in color are active. Press the house icon to return to the home page.

Using Foursquare

FOURSQUARE IS USED TO SHARE OPINIONS about establishments, services, and brands on which the community comments and evaluates publicly. Thus, if you need to choose a place to eat or find out where to buy a T-shirt, you can find out what is available close by as well as the opinions of other members. The owners can also register their businesses, make special offers, and interact in different ways with their customers through the network. In this exercise, we invite you to register your business.

1. Go to **https://es.foursquare.com/business/** to search for your business.

2. Choose the **Free Business Tools** section and click on the **Claim Your Business** link. 🗩1

3. You have to create a personal account at Foursquare and search for your business. For the moment, click on the second link, type your address into the search field, and click the **Search** button. 🗩2

4. If your place does not appear on the list that comes up, click the **Add a new place to foursquare** link. 🗩3

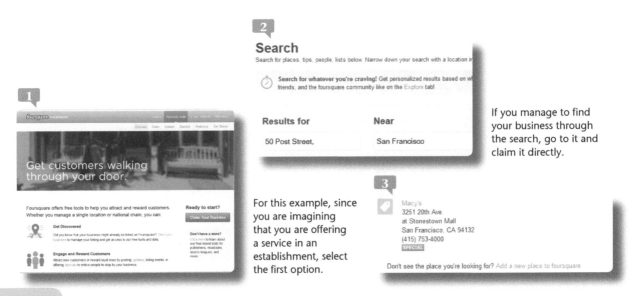

If you manage to find your business through the search, go to it and claim it directly.

For this example, since you are imagining that you are offering a service in an establishment, select the first option.

5. Log in with your Facebook account, complete all the data on the **Add Venue** page, and, when you have finished, click the **Save** option.

6. You have now registered the location. Click the **Share via E-mail** link, introduce the e-mail addresses of the people whom you would like to invite to see your profile and click the **Send** button.

7. Any user can access your business now and leave a tip or a comment about it. Click the **Claim here** link. 5

8. By paying USD$1 you can claim the business as your own, create promotions, analyze the data, and update the information about your business. You should give a telephone number so you can receive a phone call to confirm your data. 6 To see the service's potential, click the **Explore** tab at the top of the page, and in the **I'm looking for** dialog box, type the address of your business. 7

9. Places that correspond to the search conditions are displayed on the map. Place the pointer over one of them to see its label 8 and click on it for more details in the panel on the left.

10. Click on the name of the business to see its page on Foursquare and to read what customers are saying about it. 9

IMPORTANT

A yellow circular icon with a number indicates that the establishment offers promotions to Foursquare, which are displayed when a person clicks on it. Each time a user clicks an establishment's **I was here** button, they **Check in.**

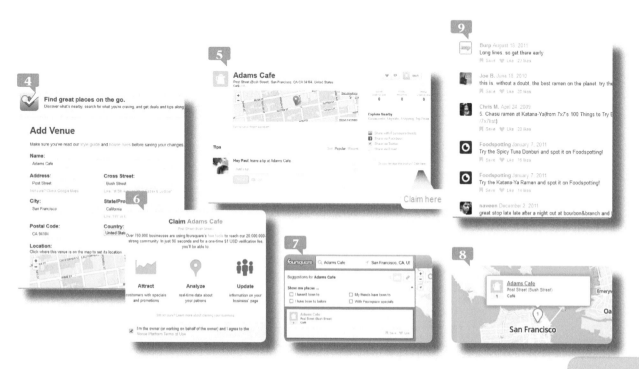

Expressing yourself through Pinterest images

WITH PINTEREST, USERS EXPRESS THEMSELVES AND communicate through virtual pinboards where they share images called pins, which can be their own or those of other users.

1. Go to the Pinterest website (www.pinterest.com), click the **Join Pinterest** button 🔲 and, using your Facebook account, 🔲 create a new Pinterest account. 🔲

2. Follow five collections of pins to get started. Do it and click on **Next**. 🔲

3. Create your first board. Choose a category, type a name, and click on the **Create Board** button. 🔲

4. On the **Following** page, users' images related to your first selection are displayed. Open the user menu and select the **Settings** option. 🔲

5. Update your account and don't to add your web page or blog address, and link your account with those of Twitter and Facebook.

6. Find friends using the method offered and save the changes.

7. Click the **Add** button in the header 🔲 and, in the box that opens, select the **Add a Pin** option. 🔲

8. Open an image that you had uploaded to Flickr or your blogs, copy its URL (by using the shortcut menu), paste it

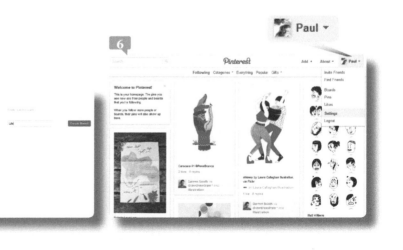

into the URL field of the **Add a Pin** box, and click the **Find Images** button.

9. Indicate the name of the pinboard on which you would like to place the photo, select the Facebook and Twitter options to share it on these applications, and click the **Pin It** button. 9

10. Click the **Add** button again and, this time, use a photo from your computer to create a new pin.

11. To the right of your pin you can see the pinboard icon. Click on it and, when it opens, click on the **Edit Board** button.

12. Fill in the details and save the settings. 10

13. Use the search field to locate images on a subject, place the pointer over an image you like (note how you can repin it), like it, or comment on it. 11 Choose the first option and add it to a new board.

14. Enhance your boards with your preferred method. 12

15. Click on your name in the top right-hand corner.

16. This will access your profile. 13 Click on the different tabs to check their content.

17. Click the Pinterest title to return to the home page. Click on the **Categories** link, choose one that interests you, and continue your journey through the images, and share those that you like.

When you pin an image, you add it to your profile.

You can pin images of your own or those of others, and also combine them on your boards.

Get the best out of the networks

AFTER LEARNING ABOUT SOME OF THE most important communication applications today, it is important for you to follow certain principles to give your page a good positioning in the search engines, as this is the most important way of reaching a wide audience.

1. It is important that the keyword with which you would like to identify your business features in the description of your page and its title. For this reason, text titles are preferable to image ones, even though the image might be the logo of your business. 🔲1

2. It is also important for the title to be concise and clear: Don't forget Twitter's 140 characters, and leave space for other information.

3. Use your business's keywords whenever possible, and it is very important to do so with your links to other websites, as well as in the subtitles to your posts and in photo and image captions. The labels h1 and h2 (for titles in levels 1 and 2) are those that best help to improve the position. 🔲2

4. Do not let an excessive use of keywords prevent you from writing in a natural manner and creating good content: Being current, useful, rich and writing with a personal tone are qualities that users and search engines favor. In the case of blogs, write posts and pages of at least 500 characters.

5. Increasing the number of pages on your site (this obviously

The title and the description are your letter of introduction. Choose carefully the texts that you will use for them to avoid having to modify them too often.

CLEARLY PAUL

16 JAN **We eat what we digest**

Just as food is the process by which eat certain products, nutrition is the process that allows us to take advantage of the nutrients in these foods. Although they are closely related, are not synonymous and, sometimes, not products we eat nourish us in the best way.

Nutrition is the action through which extract, transform and use nutrients from

increases the amount of content) improves the positioning of your site on search engines. Also, always keep a well structured menu.

6. Include on your site all the possible contact details: telephone number, e-mail address, physical address, other websites, etc.

7. Place links to your social networks in a visible place so that people can contact you easily.

8. The button for subscriptions, for following the site, and for subscribing to the feeds should be easily visible and eye-catching.

9. Do not forget to include a navigation menu that also uses the keywords of your business.

10. Be as careful with each post as you have been with the home page.

11. Set a participation calendar and stick to it to ensure that the site is dynamic. If you need to stop publishing for a while, make sure that the last shared content is particularly interesting.

12. Follow a basic code of conduct: avoid entering into controversies, be gracious toward other users, always reply to comments, and welcome newcomers.

13. Comment on other blogs and pages that are related to yours: Generating conversation is essential for creating a network.

14. Take part in other forums that are related to your subjects and offer relevant content and opinions. Do so from a public profile that includes your website's address.

IMPORTANT

Although it is important to link all of your pages, it is also important to know what to publish in each medium. Not everything that is suitable for Facebook makes sense on your blog, for example.

Allow your blog to be easily followed and shared.

To continue learning ...

IF THIS BOOK HAS MET YOUR EXPECTATIONS

This book is part of a collection that covers the most commonly used and known software in all professional areas.

All books in the series have the same approach as the one that you have just finished. If you'd like to learn more about creating your own website and promoting your business with it, do not stop here. On the next page you will find other books in the collection that may be of interest.

PHOTO EDITING

If you want to know all the secrets of the most widely used and popular program for editing images, *Learning Photoshop CS6 with 100 Practical Exercises* is undoubtedly the book you are looking for.

Photoshop is the preeminent program for photo editing and image processing. With this manual you will learn how to take advantage of its many tools and functions. In this new CS6 version of Photoshop, which is the subject of this book, Adobe has included interesting and groundbreaking developments that improve and facilitate the flow of work and increase image editing possibilities.

Using this book:

- You will get to know the new Crop in Perspective Tool.
- You will retouch images with incredible features such as Fill According to Content and the new Content-Aware Patch Tool.
- You will freely transform certain parts of an image.
- You will work on a new and spectacular 3D interface to achieve the best 3D effects.

COMPUTER-AIDED DESIGN

If you want to know all the secrets of design in one of the most valued programs out right now, *Learning Illustrator CS6 with 100 Practical Exercises* is undoubtedly the book you are looking for.

Illustrator, the vector drawing application from Adobe, is an excellent tool for computer-aided design. Thanks to its amazing and powerful features, you can create original artwork using drawings and images. Use the 100 exercises in this book to expand your knowledge and discover the thousand and one possibilities hidden in this great program.

Using this book:

- Learn about the enhanced tools for creating patterns.
- Discover the improved image tracing tool that now provides clean lines and a perfect fit.
- Apply gradients on strokes to get interesting and striking results.

OPERATING SYSTEMS

If you want to know all the secrets of the most widely used operating system, *Learning Windows 8 with 100 Practical Exercises* is undoubtedly the book you are looking for.

Windows 8 is Microsoft's new version of its operating system loaded with many new functions. You'll see the changes that Microsoft has made as soon as you start your session: A new customizable start screen that displays icons that can access the programs and applications installed on your computer. The new Metro interface of Windows 8 is specially designed to work with touch-screen devices.

Using this book:

- Get to know the Metro interface of Windows 8.
- Practice with the Ribbon in Windows Explorer.
- Work with the new and advanced Task Manager.
- Learn how to use new security and maintenance tools to always keep your PC as safe as possible.

IMAGE RETOUCH

If you want to improve the appearance of your digital photos and create amazing compositions, *Learning Image Retouch with Photoshop CS6 with 100 Practical Exercises* is undoubtedly the book you are looking for.

Photoshop is the preeminent program for retouching photographs and image processing. With the help of this manual you will learn how to use the different tools, filters, and functions in order to improve the appearance of your digital photos and create amazing compositions.

Using this book:

- Learn how to correct typical defects in photographs taken by inexperienced photographers (overexposure, underexposure, blurs, keystoning, etc.).
- Discover simple but extraordinary techniques to retouch small defects in portraits of people (dark circles, flaws, wrinkles, etc.).
- Learn how to remove people and objects.